Extreme Staff Makeover

Solutions to Recruiting, Managing, and Retaining Talent

By Dominique Molina, CPA CTC
with Bibianne U. Fell, Esq

The American Institute of Certified Tax Coaches
7676 Hazard Center Dr, Ste. 500
San Diego, CA 92108
www.CertifiedTaxCoach.org

TABLE OF CONTENTS

FOREWORD

Some of my colleagues and competitors think this book is a crazy idea. They think I am going to give away some of the best secrets top tax business owners use to efficiently staff and manage their successful practices. My response to them is simple: "You aren't seeing the bigger problem."

The problem today is small business accountants are working themselves to the bone because they can't charge enough in accounting and tax transactions to get the freedom that owning a small business is supposed to bring them.

A recent survey conducted by CPA Trendlines reports less than half of all tax practitioners are satisfied with their careers.

As a business strategy expert for accountants and tax professionals, I've coached hundreds of tax business owners across the country and have identified three easy steps to increase your job satisfaction and give you the freedom you deserve.

First, gain a designation that shows off your expertise. Examples of this are becoming a QuickBooks Professional Advisor or Certified Tax Coach™. "CPA" and "EA" are valuable marks. But they just tell people what you are – not what you do, which benefits them.

Next, get paid for your expertise by accepting fewer transaction-based engagements and more tax planning and strategy consulting agreements.

Lastly, achieve freedom by systematizing your business and giving your team an "Extreme Staff Makeover."

My goal with this book is to help tax professionals acquire the freedom that owning their own business is supposed to bring them through completely changing the way they approach hiring and managing staff.

Unfortunately, when you are studying to gain your expertise, "traditional accounting schools" don't teach you the skills necessary to attract the very best talent in the industry. Even expanding your knowledge and experience by working with one of the notorious "Big 4" firms will not give you expertise in managing your team to achieve maximum results and your desired outcomes. And, as the survey I mentioned above illustrates, less than half of tax professionals are satisfied with their job, which means even the staff you happen to catch in your business will most likely look for alternative employment relatively soon after being hired.

I've spent many years miserably in my own tax practice, and nearly four years ago, I set out to completely change the way I approach business. I developed systems, tools, processes, and techniques that have allowed me to systematize my office, work with the very best talent in the tax industry, and delegate the tasks that do not bring me utmost joy, energy, and premium revenues. I've been able to enjoy vacations during tax season, author books, accomplish dreams I'd given up long ago, become a better wife and mother and finally get paid what I'm worth because of the expertise I deliver to my tax clients. My secret resides within the way I approach running a tax business.

The problem with the tax industry today is that it is broken. Practitioners are miserable because they are forced to compete with declining fees established by low-cost chain preparation firms and "do-it-yourself" software. To increase their revenues, tax pros find themselves servicing thousands of clients in an effort to get paid the value of their expertise. The problem therein lies in the perception of the public that a tax advisor's value comes from entering data into tax software. With deadlines, increased compliance audits and notices, and more demanding clients, tax business owners find themselves trapped like I was on a never-ending hamster wheel that is their tax practices.

In 2009, I set out to change the tax industry. I began to create an elite network of tax professionals, including CPAs, EAs, attorneys and financial service providers who are trained to help their clients proactively plan and implement tax strategies that can rescue thousands of dollars in wasted tax. My more than 12 years of hands-on experience in the accounting and business fields has provided ample skills to accomplish my mission. In my role as President of The American Institute of Certified Tax Coaches™, I have successfully trained and licensed tax professionals as Certified Tax Coaches™ across the country, creating a national network of highly qualified professionals who provide proactive service for their clients. This premier group of professionals features less than 200 specialists in 40 states who have achieved this very specialized designation and learned the secrets to my success as they create their own dream tax businesses.

The American Institute of Certified Tax Coaches™ (AICTC™) is a non-profit organization dedicated to helping tax professionals establish profitable, consultative practices through tax planning. The AICTC™ is the only organization providing hands-on, proven systems, tools, and support, through a live three-day academy and a highly impactful online training program. When graduates achieve the Certified Tax Coach™ (CTC™) designation, they join a collaborative network of elite professionals who use turn-key solutions to build year-round revenues. The AICTC™ patented process results in members being empowered, valued, and respected...ultimately experiencing their dream practice.

It is my sincerest hope that you find the information and tools in this book useful and are able to use this content to enhance your tax business and goals. This, after all, is my mission: to makeover the tax industry, one tax practice at a time.

My Best Regards,

Dominique Molina

CHAPTER ONE

Acquiring Top Talent for Your Tax Business

Attracting and hiring top tax talent is one of the biggest areas of difficulty for tax business owners. Yet hiring the very best support for your business is critical to your future success. Your ability to leverage your time, focus on things you truly love to do, and grow and manage your business relies on your ability to depend on your staff to manage the lower-level functions of your day-to-day operations. For this reason, this chapter concentrates on the keys to attracting and hiring extraordinary talent for your business. I'm going to be sharing tools and practice aids so you can be a magnet for the very best in the field, and I'm going to teach you how to use systems that will lead you toward accomplishing your business goals.

To effectively run a successful tax practice, even in offices with no more than one employee, a systematic approach is crucial. Every function in a practice should be backed up by a concrete system. This is especially true if you are managing your practice to efficiently build your dream business.

Although there are many synonyms for the word "employees," such as staff or personnel, I firmly believe that the ability to build a successful business depends on the ability to bring in the very best talent. Therefore, I use the term "talent" when referring to employees. These are well-rounded employees; they have a capacity for achievement or success, they want to win, and they understand your ultimate dream of having a successful tax practice. This chapter is focused on helping you not only find these individuals, but draw them into your business and keep them there.

Unfortunately, tax business owners seem to struggle in this area, and after many years of coaching these individuals, I've found hiring, and more importantly, managing staff to get the kind of results that you want in your business are not only time consuming, they remain two of the most difficult aspects of running a tax practice.

Since time leveraging is such an important skill to master, CTC™ has developed a system for hiring. This system provides effective solutions so tax business owners can break through the barriers that are preventing them from experiencing the kind of businesses that make them want to get out of bed in the morning.

Business owners don't look forward to work each day wanting to deal with employee issues or to do all the work because they can't get the staff to do what they want them to do. Worse yet, many don't have any staff at all, because they can't find good and competent individuals who share their vision. These are all problems that stall production and negatively influence time. I will counteract all these issues by sharing a specialized hiring system, beginning with a vital element called a "Talent Profile."

Solutions

In a recent survey, AICTC™ polled tax business owners on their current satisfaction level with their office staff. While 27 percent of those polled claimed to be satisfied with their employees, 73 percent recognized that their staff was not comprised of the very best talent available. Chances are, you may also fall into the latter category. The reality is most of your peers in the tax industry are also dissatisfied with their current staff members. However, reality doesn't end there. Tax business owners want to become satisfied with their present tax staff. Most importantly, you can improve this ratio by using systems, specifically systems for attracting and hiring top tax talent.

It's even more important to use processes and systems when dealing with employees so one can more effectively delegate what I refer to as "D-level" activities. Your own definition of "D-level" activities will vary from others in your industry, but essentially a "D-level" activity is any activity that does not create energy and power for you in your business. Assigning these types of tasks and functions to the talent you've hired really leverages your time so you can do what you love to do and focus on the power activities that will advance your business into the future.

The results of the poll I shared with you above demonstrate the tremendous need for tools that allow you to start attracting and hiring top talent for your business. Therefore, we're going to focus on a six-step process to develop a personalized talent hiring system. The CTC™ Six -Step Process will guide your hiring decisions in a systemized method. When followed closely, this process will lead the very best talent to your door and allow you to identify the very best for your needs.

Step One: Developing Your TALENT Profile

Every operating business should have a business plan or a written document expressing particular goals set in advance. Your business plan acts as a roadmap to chart your course and layout the best, most direct route to your goals. Once you have a clear idea of the direction of your business, you can begin to outline your needs for accomplishing your desired results. Hiring top talent for your tax business is really no different. Beginning with a plan for hiring that corresponds to your business plan is the first step in the process to hiring the talent your business needs to carry out your vision. We call your hiring plan a TALENT profile.

The first step in the process is to create your TALENT profile. Your TALENT profile not only gives you a clear picture of who you are looking for, but it also provides the beginnings of a roadmap for the managing and retention processes, as well. When you create a solid TALENT profile deeply connected to your business plan and vision, you will be able to recognize key talent when you meet them in the attraction and hiring processes. Your TALENT profile is a clear picture of the best person that you imagine for your business need.

T The Desired Results
A Assets and Outcomes
L List Your Business Needs
E Examples of Business Goals
N Non-negotiable Requirements
T Technical Knowledge
PROFILE

A TALENT profile is very different from a job description. Job descriptions are important and will be included in your process of attracting top talent for your business, but again, your TALENT profile is not the same thing as a job description. It differs from a job description, because rather than list duties or daily functions of a particular position, a TALENT profile is not generic and is very specific to one particular position — the position particularly in your firm which will drive your company to success.

Here is an example of how a TALENT profile is different from a job description. It's one thing to say that you want a pleasant receptionist, somebody who's nice and who can greet clients at the front desk, but it's quite another thing to state you want clients to feel taken care of. You want clients who are happy to pay premium fees. You want clients to feel that they can't receive the quality of service that you provide anywhere else. Once you've listed the results that you're looking for, you start to work backwards so that you can identify the skills needed to achieve your specific desired results.

Since the profile helps you determine exactly what someone needs to accomplish to bring you success, it makes sense to start by listing the outcome you expect. The "T" in TALENT profile, therefore, stands for the Desired Results. The only reason you hire an employee is to satisfy a business need and help you accomplish your desired outcome. It is a key component of developing your TALENT profile. You can refer to your business plan or particular goals that you have for your practice when you're trying to identify your desired results.

In the AICTC™, we help our members identify specific, targeted outcomes through tax planning. Here's an example of how to use this in creating your TALENT profile. Let's say that one of your goals is to spend more time at home or to achieve a certain amount of revenues from tax planning. These desired results would be included at the start of your TALENT profile.

Perhaps your desired results include particular assets and outcomes you'd like to reach. The "A" in TALENT profile represents any particular Assets and Outcomes you desire.

When trying to identify your desired results, assets, and outcomes, your business plan enables you to reflect on your original goals and stay on track to accomplish them. Your business plan will identify your desired results, and your TALENT Profile will include additional requirements which compliment your plan.

Next, use the "L" in the TALENT profile to List your Business Needs. You might consider asking yourself the question, "What am I trying to accomplish as an organization that is not currently getting done?" Perhaps your business need is to add one more tax preparer to handle the additional work that's coming in from tax planning, or maybe you need someone to free some of your time so you can meet proactively with your clients outside of tax season. Listing your business needs in your TALENT profile allows you to keep these needs in the center of your hiring process, resulting in consistent acquisitions of talent needed to fill those needs.

Fourth, consider the "E" in TALENT profile to list examples of specific goals you have for your business. Again, you can refer to your business plan, current business goals, and personal goals in the part of the profile creation.

Try to think beyond the obvious. I gave you some examples of goals for improved revenues or time management, but think about the problems that surprisingly appear in your tax business and how solving those problems might be a goal for you. For example, clients are notorious for not giving complete information during their tax return preparation, and that's a problem. It slows down the process; there's added time involved with client follow-up. If that is a business need that appears in your business, you might reflect that need in your TALENT Profile.

Next, examine the "N" in TALENT Profile, which represents "Non-Negotiable Requirements." When evaluating a candidate to fit your TALENT profile, you have to ask yourself what this person must deliver to fulfill your business need. These requirements should be listed under the "Non-Negotiable Skills" section of the TALENT profile worksheet, as shown in Figure 1.1. Once you have an idea of what someone must accomplish to solve your need, then you can start to identify the knowledge, skills, and abilities that person needs for the position you're filling. These abilities are non-negotiable and belong in the "Vital Requirements" section of your TALENT profile.

Lastly, the second "T" in TALENT profile represents "Technical Knowledge." If your available position requires specific technical knowledge, these requirements should be listed in the "Vital Requirements" section of your TALENT profile. For example, if your business need is to delegate tax preparation in your business, you might list tax preparation experience and education as technical knowledge required for your TALENT profile.

To assist you with developing your own TALENT profile and to guide you through the process, I've included the TALENT Profile Worksheet in Figure 1.1. Make sure that you set aside the time to work on your TALENT profile. It can really make a difference in attracting the very best talent for your business and help you to recognize that talent when you see it. The TALENT profile is the cornerstone to the CTC™ Six-Step Hiring Process.

The worksheet is designed as a funnel because the combination of results, needs, knowledge, and skills are required as ingredients for your TALENT profile. Once added, your ingredients makeup the result that becomes your TALENT profile: a map to your staffing success! A complete description of a TALENT profile and sample to assist you in this process is available to CTC™ members and can be found in the CTC Toolbox™.

Figure 1.1 – TALENT Profile Worksheet

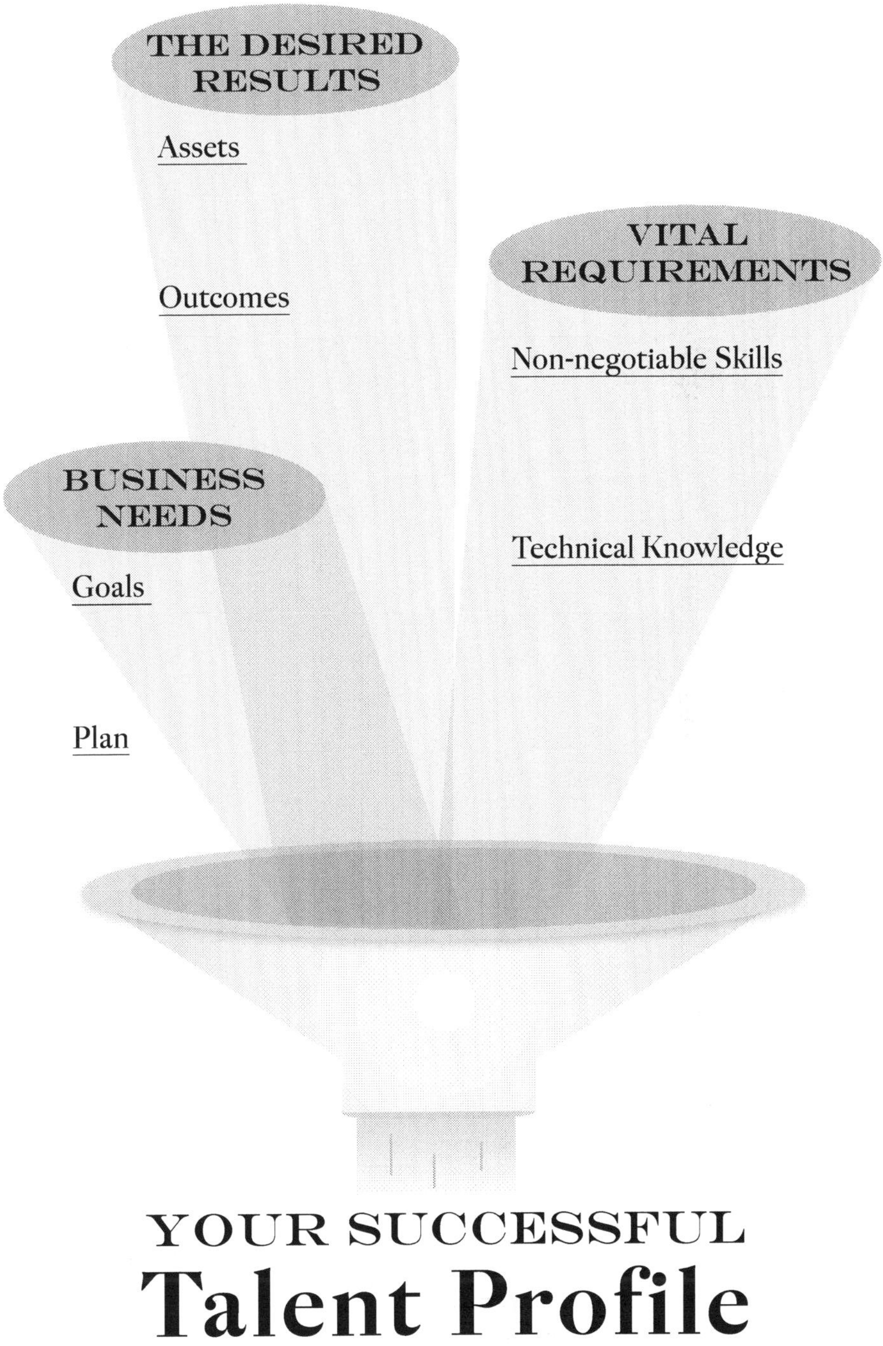

THE DESIRED RESULTS

Assets

Outcomes

VITAL REQUIREMENTS

Non-negotiable Skills

Technical Knowledge

BUSINESS NEEDS

Goals

Plan

YOUR SUCCESSFUL

Talent Profile

Section Review

According to a recent AICTC™ poll, when asked if they had ever used anything similar to a TALENT Profile to guide their hiring processes in the past, 90 percent of tax business owners admitted that they had not employed a similar process. A TALENT profile provides a clear picture of the talent you are seeking to bring you success and fill your business needs. It is a tool you can use in your tax practice to identify hiring criteria and a template for the hiring process with which you can measure candidates. It differs from a job description in that it is results driven and focused on the goals and needs of your business. Your TALENT profile will start to identify key skills and knowledge needed to accomplish your desired outcomes.

The elements of creating a profile are contained in its title:

T – The Desired Results
A – Assets and Outcomes
L – List the Business Needs
E – Examples of Business Goals
N – Non-Negotiable Requirements
T – Technical Knowledge

Step Two: Attracting and Filtering Candidates

Now that you have identified the kind of employees you need and want in your TALENT profile, you can move onto the second step of the CTC™ hiring system, which is to attract and filter candidates. This is one of the most important steps of the process, one that you should be constantly performing throughout operating your practice. You need to frequently build up your candidate pools so you can always choose from the best prospective employees, instead of complacently selecting individuals merely because they are available. Always remember, you are setting out to acquire the very best talented people who share your interests and satisfy your needs, so for this step, I'll offer some ideas on how you can construct your hiring pool. This will save you time and money and eventually leverage your abilities.

One problem that arises with this step is that candidates are everywhere and nowhere at the same time, so like most solutions in building a tax practice, there are no silver bullets to successfully build a pool of candidates. You have to use all sources available to you, whatever they may be.

Without a system in place, tax business owners frantically scrounge around to quickly get employees in the door. They are reacting to the pressure of filling the open position. Hoping that they luckily find the right person at the right time, they may even hastily make an offer that could come back to haunt them. It's ironic. As tax professionals, we approach our clients and prospects. We tell them that when it comes to taxes, it's not good enough for them to sit back and react. They need to proactively go out and take advantage of the concepts and strategies that are going to save them money before any numbers hit a 1040. The irony is most tax business owners like most business owners in general are reactive recruiters. When they have a need, they frantically scrounge around, quickly get the bodies in the door, quickly make an offer and hope the right person has made it in at the right time.

When you're trying to build a candidate pool, be aware that it doesn't happen overnight, and it requires a high amount of patience. The idea is to always be recruiting, even if you're not hiring. The very best people at hiring are the business owners who are always looking for top talent. In fact, they also have people who are constantly acting as talent scouts for them. Get your employees on board; get other referral partners to participate so essentially everyone in your practice acts like a talent scout.

It is important to work backward from your TALENT profile. Where does someone with your listed qualities hang out? Who do they socialize with? How do they socialize? Perhaps you might meet the perfect candidate at your bank, or perhaps a Chamber of Commerce meeting or other networking group. You have to get inside the mind of your ideal candidate a little bit and think about where it's possible to meet these people.

The following are a few options that will aid you to be proactive in your hiring process, allowing you the very best available talent to serve your needs.

Employee and Other Referrals

One of the best sources for finding candidates is a trusted referral. In this business, we focus on client referrals, but what we might fail to overlook is that employee referrals are just as valuable to us in the long term. Employee referrals are probably the best recruitment source because they're really cost-effective, and they build goodwill and retention with your existing staff. Since your employees spend a lot of time together, who better to judge the personality styles and potential fit than somebody who's personally referring them? If you don't have employees right now, or let's say you're unhappy with the ones that you presently have, ask other professionals you know. The referral process shouldn't be limited to just employees; they can come from anywhere as long as they're reliable. The trick is to be specific and provide a copy of your TALENT profile and a detailed job description so that the people who are looking out for you will know exactly who and what you need.

Social Networking

LinkedIn and other social media websites and blogs can also be a great way to connect with people by referral, so don't hesitate to post status updates and messages to group boards. Ask for introductions. Utilize the technology that is available to you.

College Students and Military Personnel

College campuses and government organizations provide great sources of candidates. This includes alumni associations or groups.

Extracurricular Organizations

Organizations, such as the Chamber of Commerce, conduct a lot of mixers, meetings, and networking events. Join groups with like-minded professionals and you may open yourself up to a world of candidates. You never know; you could find a potential candidate at your local golf course.

Craigslist

Craigslist is a valuable resource, because it's really cost-effective, it's expedient, it's popular, and it's easily accessible. Hundreds of responses could generate within the first day of a job advertisement's posting.

There is one catch. If you read most job listings, you'll find that most focus on the company itself. You might see a job posting that says, "This is who we are. We're going here. We're doing this. We're doing that. This is what is great about us." The truth is the candidates don't really want to know about that. Sure, it's important in the long run, but the applicant really wants to know the benefit they'll receive for working for you. The types of responses one receives from an ad that is a generic, standard, typical job posting for a tax preparer are not going to be as highly qualified as the candidates that will apply for a more precise job posting.

Therefore, another way that you can cut through unqualified candidates is by carefully crafting your job description. This technique is highly revered by CTC™ members when attracting and finding top talent for their tax businesses. What they like about this is it also really helps them to focus on the qualities that match their TALENT profile. The following is an excerpt of a detailed job description I've used in my own tax practice with much success:

> *"Looking for a world-class, part-time tax professional to team-up and support a CPA entrepreneur and author running several companies. In essence, I'm looking for someone to team-up with to help me leverage my time and create amazing business results. You'll be working from our office located eight minutes from downtown San Diego in the Mission Valley community. You must be meticulous. You have a fine eye for the details. Resourceful. You always find a way to make it work. Solution-oriented; when I give you a project or assignment, you figure out a way to make it happen. Solid people skills; able to get things done by working well with people. Able to negotiate better pricing alternatives, etc., with vendors in a way that has them feeling good about it. Flexible; you can gracefully*

handle changing priorities and effectively deal with unexpected obstacles. Hyper-organized; able to handle a large variety of projects and tasks and make sure nothing slips between the cracks. Utterly reliable. Completely trustworthy. Well-spoken, articulate; can communicate professionally and informally over the phone, in-person, and in-writing. Independent; doesn't need me to micromanage things, but instead, you excel when given clear outcomes you are responsible for and then turn loose to get them done. Always looking for ways to create systems and structure to make projects and tasks flow better and be easier for the future. A great deal of common sense and business sense. Understand at a practical level how the business works so that you can help the company minimize costs and exposures and maximize and leverage opportunities in relationships. Ability to multitask; you'll be handling multiple projects and tasks across a broad front, so you'll need to be able to move and insure that nothing is missed. A fearless leader; able to supervise a level two tax preparer who has routine questions and catch what they don't know. Problem and project owner; you take charge of the project and work independently to see a project through to its completion; you don't need anyone telling you to start the next step in the process, rather, you consistently complete projects from start to finish. Comfortable with technology and able to learn new software skills; expert level proficiency at Word, Excel, Outlook, QuickBooks, and other software. Ability to leap over hurdles of incomplete data by gathering information necessary to prepare and complete an accurate return; this includes strong organization skills and forethought to consider what may be missing. . ."

What I liked about the responses that I received from a posting like that is that they were more highly qualified. Having a detailed job description, such as the one I use in my tax practice, is one way you can filter your applicants. Get specific, and use your TALENT profile to build your description so you can cut down on the unqualified responses.

Another way that you can cut through the unqualified candidates is by making a specific request in order for the candidate to apply. This is one of my top secrets in tracking and finding stars for my tax business. In my job posting, I request that the candidate send me a detailed letter explaining how they fit with my detailed job description in the posting. It's very simple. Anyone who doesn't follow my instructions is thrown out of the pool. So if I receive a resume or a plain, generic, cover letter, I don't even look at it. This cuts down on my time spent reviewing candidates. What CTC™ members like about this technique is it really helps the candidate to focus on their qualities that match your TALENT profile. It can tell you right away if you've found someone you want to invest more time in exploring.

Step Three: Preparing Interview Questions

Now that you've found a few candidates who fit your TALENT profile, the third step is to invite them for an interview. In preparation for this assessment, because that's what an interview is – an assessment of prospective employees – you must organize relevant interview questions to ask candidates when they arrive.

It really doesn't matter if you're sitting across the desk from the absolute best person for your job opening or if you're sitting across from the worst one, if you don't use effective interview questions, you won't be able to identify the true talent for your business. Therefore, the goal is to gather as much information as possible in a short amount of time.

There are four parts of developing interview questions: they should be easy to answer, they should only have one answer, they should have a planned, specific purpose, and they should be job-related. As you prepare your interview questions, keep in mind what piece of information you are looking for when you ask that question. Design your questions to elicit that piece of critical information.

When you're writing your interview questions, make sure to ask questions that will confirm that a candidate is able to perform similarly to the needs you have identified in your TALENT profile.

Step Four: Conducting the Interview

The fourth step is to direct the face-to-face interview. Because leveraging your time and assets is such an important element of the

AICTC™, leverage is especially relevant for the actual interview. You need to maintain control of the interview, get the information you need, sell the person on the position, and conclude the interview in a timely fashion. If you can do these things effectively, you've conducted a successful interview.

I use the active term, "direct the interview," when describing the process. As the director of the interview, you need to maintain control of the interview so that you can get the information you need. You can take charge of the interview with the questions you prepared in the third step.

An important part of the interview is initially telling the candidate exactly what's going to happen during the interview and in the order it's going to occur. This compliments the theory of using systems in your hiring process. By performing the interview using a systematic approach, you will accomplish more; you will obtain more information in a shorter amount of time.

Taking notes is also a critical part of the interview. You can use your notes as a reference point. Ultimately, it will help you evaluate your candidate in relation to your TALENT profile.

The next thing you should strive to do is sell the job at the end of the interview. By the end of the interview and using the information you gathered during it, you'll realize how to present the job to this particular person. This works especially well if you're on a shoestring budget. If you're working on a limited budget in the amount of salary or compensation package that you can offer the candidate, you now know enough at the end of the interview to sell that job, focusing on other features and benefits you can offer working with your firm. I'll be discussing more ideas and strategies for creative compensation later in this book.

Last, your TALENT profile will help you conclude an interview more swiftly. Knowing your needs and requirements beforehand will greatly determine whether or not you're interested in a candidate and if you should either shorten or lengthen the actual interview. If a candidate does not conform to your TALENT profile, you can save time by concluding the interview ahead of schedule. There is no need to conduct lengthy interviews if it is clear that your candidate does not match your TALENT profile.

Step Five: Investigate Data

The fifth step in the process is to investigate the information you gathered while interviewing a candidate. In this step, you virtually become a police detective. The point of the interview is for you to obtain quality data in order to make a worthwhile decision, but the quality of the data is only as good as the truthfulness of it. Thus, you have to research the information and confirm its validity before you can make a final decision.

This step is pretty straight-forward. You want to ask candidates for references and then actually make contact with those references. You want to perform a background check and verify candidates' employment histories.

In this part of the process, you need to be a good sleuth. Get creative so that you can verify the data that you have. For example, when you contact a candidate's references, ask those references for others who may know the candidate. These are called secondary references, and they can provide a more neutral opinion of the person. When a candidate gives you a reference to contact, it's probable he or she is someone they know really well. They also know the person's going to give them a very high recommendation. As a result, that person may be biased in the favor of the candidate. Asking for a secondary reference can get you a more neutral opinion of the candidate that you're evaluating and help alleviate that bias. However, be aware that you'll need to have a candidate sign a disclosure indicating that you're going to ask for secondary references. As with most business decision making, especially when dealing with employees, make certain that you're within legal parameters. I'll discuss more about legal requirements later in this book.

Step Six: Making a Decision

The last step of the CTC™ Six-Step Hiring Process is making the final decision based on your TALENT profile, and this is the most critical part of the process. It is important because you're relying on how well you have fulfilled the first five steps of this process to make a choice that will affect the outcome of your business.

You should always make decisions between the candidates you have interviewed compared to your TALENT profile. I strongly suggest using a scoring matrix to evaluate your candidates. Scoring your candidates provides a more definitive assessment and can determine the best talent of two or more highly qualified candidates. I must stress however, that you are not comparing your candidates against each other. Conversely, you are scoring the candidates against your TALENT profile. This often missed element makes the difference between hiring someone reactively, which you want to avoid, and proactively seeking the best talent for your business needs and desired outcomes.

A sample scoring matrix is available for CTC™ members and can be found in the CTC Toolbox™. The scoring matrix grades candidates according to your TALENT profile's guidelines.

Common Traps

- **Picking up a resume a couple of minutes before a candidate arrives at your office for an interview.**
  This is a reactive response and is inconsistent with using a systematic approach to improve your abilities to attract and hire top talent for your tax business. Recall the first and third steps of our hiring system. A TALENT profile will remind you of what you need in a candidate, and preparing relative interview questions will help support the information contained in the TALENT profile and candidate's resume. Always go into an interview well prepared.

- **Letting referrals be your only source for your hiring pool.**
  Take into account that although referrals are an excellent way of expanding your hiring pool, they are not the only tactic available to you. Be open to as many possibilities as possible. Cast a wide net of methods to gather candidates. Remember, there are no silver bullets in the hiring process.

- **Asking trick questions during an interview.**
  I know that there are some real elaborate interview questions out there, but we're not psychologists, and it doesn't make any sense to spend your time with someone who can't answer your trick ques-

tions. You're not going to get the information that you need if the person you're interviewing is confused by the question or has to think through many answers so that they can provide the best one to you. You are looking for authentic answers during an interview, so ask authentic questions.

- **Making a decision about a candidate during the first five minutes of an interview.**
  Statistics show that more than 80 percent of interviewers make up their mind about a candidate in the first five minutes of the interview. The fact is you just can't gather enough information in those five minutes to make an accurate decision. Always stick to your TALENT profile when making a decision. If you find yourself making a decision within a short time frame, you know you have not gathered enough information to score a candidate against your TALENT profile.

- **Making the most common hiring mistake of all: evaluating candidates against one another.**
  Business owners tend to pit candidates against one another, as if the hiring process is a competition. Unfortunately, this is very unproductive. Comparing each candidate to your TALENT profile, not to another candidate, will ensure that you hire top talent for your tax business. Your TALENT profile is the path to finding winners.

Frequently Asked Questions

- **Would you use the Star Profile for part-time or seasonal staff hiring?**
  Absolutely. The point of this whole process is that it's systematized. The reason why having a system for this is so important is because it helps you to become an expert at the hiring process, whether you're looking for full-time, part-time, seasonal, or even temporary employees. You want to follow a routine so that you can build efficiency and effectiveness. This works especially well for seasonal staff hiring, because you're doing it over and over again, and

if you're repeating the same steps the same way, you're going to get better and better at it. As a result, you'll be able to make your decisions accurately and quickly.

- **Does the TALENT Profile apply to virtual employees?**
  In the same way that the system applies for part-time or seasonal help, the system works just as well for virtual help. What you want to see from virtual employees is their experience as virtual employees and success stories where they've made it work. Virtual employment offers some specific challenges that you don't find in a traditional "nine-to-five" position. I've had successful experiences with virtual employees in the past, as have many of CTC™ members across the country. Make sure to tailor your TALENT profile to coincide with the guidelines you think you need for successful virtual employees, and you'll be ready to screen potential virtual candidates!

- **What if I have an employee who has a good work ethic, but he or she wants perks that other employees don't have?**
  You can also use your TALENT profile to assess existing staff. You need to evaluate your current staff and rate them as to how they compare to your TALENT profile. This tool is going to give you some guidance on the systems you need to develop to make your working relationship more efficiently and motivate your staff to do the job that you want them to do. It will also give you valuable information for evaluating that person in performance reviews and perhaps you may discover they're not the right fit for your business. When you are armed with this information, you can decide if offering additional perks and benefits is worth the investment the staff member making the request. If an employee is extremely valuable and meets your TALENT profile exceptionally, you might want to maintain that relationship and extend exceptional benefits to that stellar employee. Your TALENT profile will help you determine the value of your employee.

- **Is it acceptable to have another person sit-in on an interview?**
  If you have other staff members in your office who you feel would

add value to the hiring process, they may be a great resource to have during an interview. The question you need to ask yourself if you're considering whether or not to include other interviewers in the process is what value do they add to the hiring system? Do they have a particular skill that will enable them to be a better judge of that characteristic in the candidate? Interviewing in-tandem could actually be a great advantage. On the other hand, merely having a second person sit in on interviews without adding value can be a waste of resources and can actually slow down the evaluation process.

- **I'm a sole proprietor. What advice do you have as to when to start hiring staff and expanding my practice?**
  Remember to start with and refer to a business plan outlining the current and future needs of your practice. Also, recall your business need as determined in your TALENT profile. These steps are very important. You should refer to your business plan, look at your goals, and be results-oriented, and then, when you can identify your needs, you can start to outline what sort of staffing you need to make those desired results happen.

DID YOU KNOW?

Current statistics suggest that on average, hiring the wrong person for the job costs an organization at least 2-1/2 times the employee's salary. This doesn't include less measurable costs, such as low morale and loss of customers.[1]

Chapter One in Review

Hiring the very best support for your business is critical to your future success. The CTC™ Six-Step Hiring Process provides effective solutions so tax business owners can break through the barriers that are preventing them from experiencing the kind of businesses they've always dreamed of operating.

The following steps of this hiring process were addressed in this chapter.

- **Step One: Developing Your TALENT Profile.**
  Your TALENT profile paints a clear picture of the best candidates you imagine for a position in your tax practice to fulfill your business need. When you create a solid TALENT profile deeply connected to a previously written business plan that expresses the goals and visions of your company, you will be able to recognize key talent when you meet them in the attraction and hiring processes. Different from a general job description, a TALENT profile measures:
    - The Desired Results;
    - Assets and Outcomes;
    - List Your Business Needs;
    - Examples of Business Goals;
    - Non-Negotiable Requirements, and;
    - Technical Knowledge.

- **Step Two: Attracting and Filtering Candidates.**
  Once the kind of employees you need and want in your TALENT profile is identified, you can move onto one of the most important steps of the process, one that should be performed long before and after the hiring process is complete. Always be recruiting; you never know when you'll need to access your candidate pool, and you never want to rush into hiring individuals who are merely available. Some methods of attracting top talent for your practice are:

  - Employee and Other Referrals;
  - Social Networking;
  - College Students and Military Personnel;
  - Extracurricular Organizations, and;
  - Job Boards, such as Craigslist.

- **Step Three: Preparing Interview Questions.**
  Develop questions that will answer whether or not a candidate truly fits your TALENT profile. These questions should have four elements:

  - They should only have one answer.
  - They should be easy to answer.
  - They should have a planned, specific purpose.
  - They should be job-related.

- **Step Four: Conducting the Interview.**
  As the conductor of an interview, you must explain to a candidate exactly what's going to happen during the interview and in the order it's going to occur. Similarly to how you sell the value of your business to tax clients, you should sell its value to prospective employees. Again, follow your TALENT profile closely when performing an interview, and at all costs, avoid prematurely making a decision.

- **Step Five: Investigate Data.**
  Become a detective in regards to the information you gather from an interview. Get creative. For example, ask a candidate's reference for other possible references. This broadens the scope of opinions you'll receive on the interviewee.

- **Step Six: Making a Decision.**
  Effectively make a decision based on your TALENT profile. Remember, never compare candidates against each other; this is a reactive approach. Rather, evaluate proactively, which can be done with the methods discussed in this chapter, such as a scoring matrix.

CHAPTER TWO

Managing Employees and Systemizing Your Office

This chapter on managing staff to get the kind of results you really want in your business is going to help you get more done in less time with the kind of quality that you really want to deliver to your clients.

By now, you're well aware of my fondness of systems. Now, you may be saying to yourself that your office knows how to conduct itself and you know how to run day-to-day procedures, but if your systems are not documented, you do not have a "leveragable" asset.

Systems are really the true building blocks of a successful business. Most tax practice owners might think that systems are only necessary for larger businesses — perhaps a business with a lot of employees or multiple offices. However, I want to express how systems make a difference for even a "solopreneur," or a boutique-sized firm. Systems are the only way to leverage your skills and your time, and at the same time, ensure quality in an environment where quality control on the technical aspects of your work can mean legal liability and even penalties from government regulators. Technical accuracy is extremely critical in today's world. Controlling the details through systems is going to allow you to take a higher-level role and focus more on running the business, rather than just working as an employee in your own practice.

Documenting your processes and systematizing your business not only adds value to your business for resale, it really lets you leverage your time and experience economies of scale to flourish today. The goal of this chapter is to help you see the value of systematizing your business and also provide you with the tools that you need to begin implementation in your office immediately.

The Process of Systematizing

Systematizing may seem like an overwhelming undertaking at first, but here is some good news: the tax industry offers so many opportunities to systematize processes. This may be contrary to what you might think because of the technical nature and expertise required in a tax business, but it is because of the critical importance that your work be technically correct that you must have systems for completing the work.

Although 81 percent of recently polled tax practitioners told us that they currently utilize systems in their offices, 19 percent replied they do not. Further, of those who reportedly do use systems in their business, perhaps only a fraction of those actually document their systems. My goal is to raise this percentage to 100 percent of our nation's tax business owners, who will completely systematize and back up their processes with adequate documentation. Raising awareness and providing solutions through the AICTC™, along with the tools and information outlined in this book are some of the ways we can promote change in our industry. Wouldn't it be great to leverage your time, effectively motivate your team to do exceptional and quality work, and raise the standard of accuracy in our industry? Systematizing your business is the way to accomplish this mission.

The AICTC™ offers its members The CTC Systems Roadmap™, which is a proven seven-step process that effectively systematizes each method within a tax practice.

The Financial Impacts of Systems

Generally speaking, systems will be the primary money saver for your business. It's basic financial defense. Your chief money maker (financial offense) will be your marketing and how you position yourself as an expert in proactive tax planning. For CTC™ members, this means eliminating your competition because you are a Certified Tax Coach™ and your competitors are not. But it is your systems that will help you save the most in your business. Without systems, your expenses just happen without justification. With systems and processes, expenses are something you actively control and continually reduce.

You can use systems to control your labor expense. For most tax business owners, labor tends to be the biggest discretionary expense. Systematizing the tax process, or any other process for that matter, creates efficiency. With tax procedures in particular, the more you can simplify the process and remove some of the judgment of lower level staff, the more efficiently they'll work, and that saves you money in the long term.

Other Benefits of Systems in a Tax Practice

Any time that you have a repetitive task, you can easily create systems to handle those tasks. Consequently, your business will run more smoothly and you and your staff will consume less time on mundane tasks.

Having systems in place ensures quality and reduces errors. As I previously mentioned, because of the importance of technical competence in the tax industry, tax practitioners need to have systems in place to avoid critical errors. Essentially, it is through the use of systems that you can raise the quality and accuracy of your work.

You can use systems to handle the challenge of variables in your business. In the tax industry, there are many types of variables in your day-to-day operations. Variables are problems. They're problems because they're unexpected and uncontrollable events. The biggest variable that is exceedingly difficult to control is the people involved with your practice. We've all experienced stress, either financially-related from clients not paying or deadline-related from clients not providing timely information. You're never going to be able to predict what's going to happen or preplan for every situation, but using systems in your office can help control the outcome and really train your clients on how they must behave if they want to remain one of your clients.

Reduce unnecessary stress caused by the nature of the tax industry by implementing systems. Much of the benefits that we've talked about will be for you as the business owner. For example, reduced expenses, improved efficiency, and the ability to leverage your time are all advantages, but you're also going to find that implementing systems in your office improves retention for your staff.

Systems really provide a framework for your employees to succeed, because as a manager, you're fostering an environment of success. You provide the structure and that really allows your team to excel. Unhappy employees create unwarranted stress in your tax practice, as well as your personal life.

Systems improve employee performance and morale. When you can create an attractive environment for your employees, one in which they're allowed to excel, one in which you purposely implement procedures to increase efficiency and reduce stress, that becomes attractive, and you'll be able to retain top talent.

Reiterated, no business is too small for systems. If you're a one-man shop ("solopreneur"), if you use independent contractors, or use seasonal or part-time employees, you need systems.

Furthermore, if you use virtual employees, systems are non-negotiable. If you're managing an environment where you're not able to see your employees due to a virtual arrangement, you must have some way to implement consistency and to ensure quality of work. Systematizing your business can do that for you and provide tools so you can manage your business from anywhere in the world.

Assessing Your Business

You need to have a willingness to honestly assess your business. Simply saying that you're satisfied with complacently repeating actions year after year, such as earning the same annual salary, and running your business in the same manner is not going to improve your practice. Humbly look at your business with fresh eyes so you can make real improvements where they are needed.

In addition, for this process to work, you must have a bird's-eye view on what happens in your office.

Most of the time, as managers, we have no idea the level of problems that exist until we ask. For example, you should consider an end-of-tax season debriefing. Tax business owners tend to focus on simply surviving workloads, meeting deadlines, and collecting revenue during tax season. After the first debrief, one could find that his or her unavailability to staff due to a busy schedule was making their jobs difficult and making the team miserable. They don't know how to communicate with their boss, they didn't want to bother him or her, and so they hold back. These employees might have been sitting on work because they were stuck until they could find their leader approachable.

When you're unapproachable to your staff, much inefficiency occurs. You need to work with your employees to create a system for communication in your office. Set aside a short amount of time each week with your staff members so that you can discuss their workloads and any questions they have. Again, utilize what's available to you. For instance, implement physical mailboxes for messages for files to review and/or adopt an interoffice instant messaging system for quick questions so employees don't have to leave their desks.

As a result, you'll find increased communication and efficiency on all of your tax work, and the staff will be so much happier. In return, this will improve office morale. This will also ensure use of the processes and the systems, as well. When you've got buy-in from your staff because they were a part of creating a system, they'll be more likely to actually follow that system.

Another way to critically assess your business is through networking. Consider joining a mastermind group and allow your peers to ask you tough questions about your business systems. You may be presented with issues you hadn't previously pondered. Collaboration is a wonderful benefit when advancing your tax practice. It's nice to have someone outside your business to ask you the tough questions you're afraid of asking yourself. Do your systems make sense? As a final benefit, when you state your goals to other people, you're more motivated to accomplish them.

Once you've thoroughly assessed your practice, you're ready to begin the seven-step process; I call it "The CTC™ Systems Roadmap."

Step One to Systematizing: Identify What You'd Like to Improve

In the first step to systematization, list the aspect of your practice that you'd like to improve. These could include workflow obstacles, invoicing issues, etc. The items on your list can be fixed through proper systems.

In a recent AICTC™ poll, 96 percent of tax businesses polled indicated that they can immediately recognize aspects in their businesses that they would like to improve. If you can realize portions of your business that you would like to change, you are not alone. Start to identify what you need to change in order to become a better business.

To help you identify the things you'd like to improve, consider things that may have big financial impacts or things that cause you much unwarranted pain.

For purposes of illustrating this process for you, I'll lead you through an example as we discuss the seven steps to creating a system. For my example, I'll use my very own Systems Roadmap that I created for my business over three years ago. For step one, I listed "workflow," as the aspect that I'd like to improve.

Step Two of Systematizing: Identify Current Problems

Step two is a more in-depth analysis of the aspects of your business that you'd like to improve. What are the current processes that you're using, and what problems arise because of them? Step two focuses on listing these problems.

Realize that success and professional growth depend on systematization. It's neither personality nor technical skill that really ensures your success and growth. You can be the most popular or intelligent tax practitioner in the country, but those characteristics don't ensure you having the most effective business systems and processes. Also, note that these processes aren't meant to belittle or patronize your staff; they will actually empower them to do an excellent job for you.

To continue with my example of "workflow," in step two I listed, "Files are all over the office; one person may have several projects pending, while reviewers are waiting idly for work; you don't know if you actually realized the profit on any given project, and; time is wasted searching all over the office to locate a file." Do any of my past problems sound familiar to you?

Step Three of Systematizing: Identify Solutions

Step three requires you to identify potential solutions to your problem. This is a brainstorming exercise for potential solutions. After you've identified what you want to change and the problems associated with those aspects, write down the potential solutions to each issue.

In my example of "workflow," I felt that tracking mechanisms might possibly be a solution to the problem. I listed "tracking mechanisms," to solve both the problem of file location and status of projects, as well as the profitability of projects.

I also listed "Work in Process (WIP) worksheets, so work can be reassigned and also, a clear process for the physical route a tax return takes in the office." I felt that having defined procedures for the physical location of files would assist in being able to locate them more quickly.

At this point in the process, you won't have all the answers, it is meant to inspire a collection of potential solutions to your problem.

Step Four of Systematizing: The "Sticky-Noting Process"

The next step in the process is what I call the "Sticky-Noting Process", and it basically entails writing down each step of every process as you complete it. When creating systems in your business, consider the steps required as if you are performing the tasks yourself. This process works especially well if you can complete it as you perform the task. Document each step of the process on a sticky note. You can place the sticky notes in order up on a board to summarize processes in your system. This is a creative outline for defining a system.

To continue my "workflow" example, my "Sticky-Noting Process" might consist of, "Return preparation, return review, clearing review notes, performing second reviews, etc." Everyone will have a different "Sticky-Noting Process," because everyone will have various systems in place according to the specific needs of their businesses.

Step Five of Systematizing: Controlling the Variables

Variables are all the things that can change and affect your tax practice. The fifth step asks you to identify these occurrences so you can develop a plan to handle them effectively. If you offer tax planning in your business, you will recognize this step as analogous to what you do when you create a tax plan for a client.

People tend to be the biggest variable in a tax business, such as when they fail to provide the information we need to prepare their tax returns. Another major issue is staff being out of the office unexpectedly. This can create obstacles to the workflow.

For purposes of my "workflow" example, I listed people as one of my variables. Here is what I documented for step five: "Missing information, staff out of the office, clients who haven't paid, staff not updating their assignment lists, staff not using systems, etc."

As I was working on this step in my example three years ago, I began to realize potential variables in the new process I was developing. I identified new potential variables, such as, "Employees not using systems," in anticipation of potential obstacles to my new process. By recognizing potential barriers to your new system, you can anticipate them and include steps to overcome these variables in your process.

Think of this as creating a workflow plan for yourself. When you have predetermined systems in place, variables will be less likely to negatively impact your business operations.

Step Six of Systematizing: Designing a Plan

Step six presents you with the opportunity to design a plan to handle the variables you've identified in step five. Your plan is literally a preemptive attack against variables. This stage of the process highlights the importance of preparedness. The system you develop will thwart obstacles and keep your process running as smoothly as possible.

My plan to combat the variables in my example are, "Place projects with missing information in a special bin, task the administrators with calling those clients daily to follow up on projects in the pending bin, use work in process listings and desk bins to reassign work when staff is out of the office, place projects in a separate location for non-paid clients, and implement a pay-up-front policy."

Whenever possible, it is better to avoid the obstacle in the first place than have a better system for dealing with the obstacle. Consider variable avoidance in your plan design.

Step Seven of Systematizing: Measurement

The seventh step of the process addresses measurement and accountability. Systems are nearly meaningless without tracking.

I'm getting back to basics here when I discuss measurement, but it's a bit like some of the clients we've all worked with who have businesses and don't have a clue how much money they've made. Has that ever happened to you? You work with a client, you do all their QuickBooks data entry at the end of the year, and they didn't have a clue all year how much money they've made.

I personally can't imagine not knowing how much money I'm making, but I'm continually amazed when I see clients who just have not a clue. Success really can't be determined if you don't track your performance accordingly; focus on tracking performance in key areas.

Determining which areas of your tax business are important will vary from person to person. Your key areas can be anything depending on which aspect of your business you're focusing on and they can change with time if you find that what you're measuring is no longer relevant to your business or process.

You can identify priorities in your own business. For instance, in a tax practice, you may be interested in measuring levels of service efficiency and of course profitability. For measuring levels of service, you can use client evaluations; you can use your client retention numbers year after year to measure your level of service and your employees' levels of service. For efficiency, you can measure productivity per employee, quantity of projects, project realization, and quality of work through staff reviews.

In order to ensure accurate measurement of results, you need a system for collecting and tracking your data. These can come in many different forms, such as spreadsheets or manually tracking your information. It can also come from specialized software, such as operational software for tracking projects. There are great project management software packages available to assist you in tracking workflow and profitability in your business.

When you're considering how to implement those measurement systems, you need to think about tax season or other utterly hectic times of the year. Your focus should be on the easiest way to get that data on a regular basis, despite a chaotic environment.

Completing step seven requires that you start to develop some ideas on ways that you can measure results. Really focus on the results that you have in mind, and then project backwards on how you can track those types of results successfully.

Continuing my example of "workflow," I listed, "Use of operational software to track workflow and profitability, as well as the location of the files." I also listed, "Development and use of a dashboard to track key results and staff performance reviews based on measured results."

You can start to develop benchmarks and standards for each area you measure in your business. Begin by looking at your past performance data if you have it available, or you can use your own goals.

You may not have past performance data available. If you're new in the business, or if you haven't been tracking some of these key areas before, you may not have past performance data available. In this case, what you might want to do is aim low first and then start with your goal. Set a goal and be reasonable about that goal. If you don't have historical data to start with, just use your goal, but no matter what you use as a benchmark, you'll need to refine your standards over time so that you can continually improve your business.

Implementing measurement tools in your business really requires the ability to see where you're going. I recommend developing a dashboard for your business so you have a routine place to check your results. A dashboard is simply your key indicators featured in one location, whether the method is software, reports, or listing on a bulletin board.

It is so important to be able to identify and review your key areas in a moment's notice. When you implement this level of measurement, you own the types of tools that allow you to run your business from the beach. Frankly, no one likes the thought of adding additional responsibilities to their plate, but if you can do it in a leveraged way, it actually frees you; it's very liberating. Having the ability to instantly review your key areas through the use of systems can free your time to work on other things, spend more time with your family, even work from anywhere in the world!

Figure 2.1

SYSTEMS ROADMAP

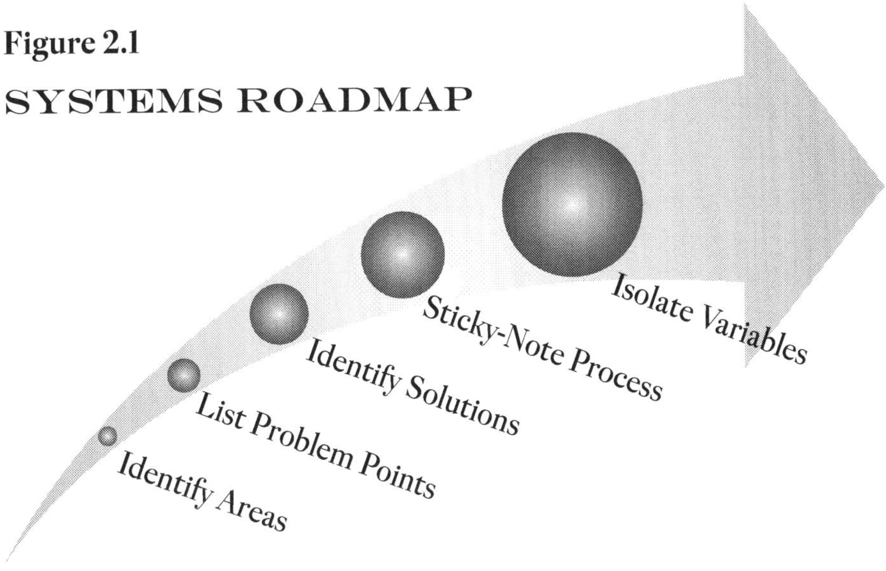

Identify Areas
List Problem Points
Identify Solutions
Sticky-Note Process
Isolate Variables

Communicating the CTC Systems Roadmap to Your Staff

Finally, you need to clearly communicate your measurement concepts to your employees. This sets a performance standard for your staff and it lays the foundation for their accountability.

Management should not be about trapping your employees or catching them doing things they aren't supposed to do; it's about building the team. You want to enable your employees to really succeed. When your employees succeed, you will accomplish your business goals. The encouragement is going to build your business, while making your staff feel happy and fulfilled. Involve your staff by clearly communicating each measurement concept to them.

You should incorporate evaluating your performance and the performance of your staff into your weekly routine. It doesn't do you any good to measure your results in a particular area, only to realize that unchanged information months later. Tax business owners are all guilty of delaying the analysis of business performance, especially during tax season. How many of you reading this actually review your key areas in real time, weekly during tax season? I can tell you, quite honestly for me, several years ago, I was not doing that, and in the beginning, I wasn't doing it at all. Later in my career, as I tried to make improvements in my business, I was reviewing performance in the summertime. After several months time, your information is just not meaningful. It is imperative to develop a habit of evaluating your performance on a weekly basis. It's especially bad if you've got a problem that's continuing to happen before you realize it. If you're not checking your key indicators for months at a time, the problem can repeat and incessantly persist. In the meantime, all those months that you remain unaware, your problems continue unnecessarily. Step seven requires a change in your own behavior so that you can act like a business navigator and not just an employee in your own business.

As I previously pointed out, taking charge of your business allows you to work ON your business rather than just IN it.

Frequently Asked Questions

- **How do I know which operational software to choose from when dealing with virtual employees?**
  Make sure to research all of your options before making a decision. Usually, software programs will have demos available to customers. Whatever you decide to implement is your solution for working with virtual employees.

  Another piece of advice would be to centralize your projects and files. You need to be working from the same server, so if you're doing cloud computing and you've got a server hosted elsewhere, you need one central location where everybody can log into, allowing you to post messages that will be viewed by everyone in your practice. There's too much room for error in only emailing. Centralizing files creates much more efficiency.

- **Do you know of an easy way to compute realization if you no longer use timesheets because you started using value billing?"**
  I prefer value billing versus billing based on time. Billing for your expertise allows you to charge what you're worth and the ability to enjoy the freedom that owning a tax business is supposed to bring you. If you're fee quoting, you'll be able to do this. When you're quoting a fee, you're just not tying it into time, so you can still calculate realization the old fashioned way if you have that information available. If you're not using timesheets anymore, you can track revenue per project. You can look at your labor costs as a percentage of your revenue. These are a few ideas on how to measure realization if you're no longer tracking hours via timesheets.

- **Are systems put into a notebook and then provided to each employee? How are they dispersed?**
  For your tax practice, you can create an operational handbook that outlines all the systems and processes that you use. You can also have frequent employee training meetings to discuss new processes and procedures. In addition, an annual tax season kick-off meeting to review every system in the office can be an effective way of

communicating systems to your staff. This would also be ideal in providing feedback for your current systems and processes.

- **Can a system simply consist of collecting bank statements, opening envelopes, performing bank reconciliations, entering adjustments, etc.?**
  Yes and no. While you should have a system for every process in your practice, you should get even more specific than just listing duties. For example, when you list "perform bank reconciliations," you might want to break that into smaller steps, such as "identify every deposit that's been posted," or, "identify every check that's been posted." Get as specific as you can. Some of the most successful businesses in the world, regardless of size, practice systematizing their processes. By following suit, you could be one of them.

DID YOU KNOW?

"Statistics show that a well-written business plan can dramatically increase your chance of success. Poor planning is the number one cause for small business failures."[2]

Chapter Two in Review

Let's briefly review the facets of success with systems.

The first one is being able to see the big picture.

Second, accept that success and growth depend on systematization. It's not personality or technical skill that really ensures your success and growth. You can be the funniest tax guy in America or the smartest tax lady in the country, but that doesn't ensure leveraged business systems and processes. Your processes aren't meant to belittle or patronize your staff; nevertheless you are empowering them to do an excellent job for you.

Lastly, have a guide separate from you asking you tough questions about your business systems. This can be a networking group. It can be a mastermind group, which is something that I particularly recommend, or even an individual accountability partner.

As I discussed in Chapter Two, The CTC™ Systems Road-Map consists of seven steps:

- Identifying what you'd like to improve;
- Identifying current problems in your practice;
- Identifying solutions to these issues;
- Practicing the "Sticky-Noting Process";
- Expecting and counter-striking variables;
- Develop a plan to fight obstacles in your practice, and;
- Track your performance and systems through proper measurement.

It's important to understand that employing systems without tracking and measurement is counterproductive. You need to incorporate evaluating your performance into your weekly routine. It doesn't do you any good to measure your results in a particular area and learn of a problem, only to see that problem recurred months later, because you didn't evaluate for a long period of time. It's especially bad if you've got a problem that's continuing to happen before you realize it, so if you're not checking that information for months at a time, the problem can repeat and continue on and on all of those months that you remain unaware.

The most important message from this chapter is for you to change your own behavior so that you can really act like a business navigator of your practice and not just a staff member in your own business.

CHAPTER THREE

Accountability: Keeping Star Employees in Your Tax Business

Accountability can increase your staff's performance, which will lead to happier employees and help retain the very best talent in your practice. The intent of this chapter is to identify the benefits of accountability systems, as well as share ideas with you for staff appreciation, morale builders, and ultimately how to retain your top talent with non-conventional compensation, even if you're on a shoestring budget.

I want to encourage you to reinvent your business with an accountability frame of mind.

Let's start by explaining a few negatives as demonstrated in Figure 3.1. First, there is really no point to having accountability without measurement. Throughout this book, I've been sharing with you tools to help you measure your staff's performance and key factors in your business. Yet it is up to you to use the tools you have to improve your business.

Next, the majority of employee management does not come naturally to most business owners. They don't teach hiring and firing in tax accounting school. Since it doesn't tend to fit in "normal" business processes, most people simply just don't do it. It's especially important if something is not in your natural skill set to follow a system for it.

The last obstacle that I'll mention is that no one really likes confrontation. Developing a system for accountability eliminates the confrontation. I learned this technique way back when I first became a supervisor for one of the big firms. I learned from a great mentor of mine that if you can get someone to agree to a specific performance and behavior when the going is good, all you have to do later when the going gets tough is remind the person of their previous agreement. You're no longer susceptible to argument over what the person agreed to do, because you already received that agreement upfront before there's conflict. You can always bring the argument back around to what they initially agreed to do. When that person fails to do what they agreed to do, you have predesigned consequences and there's no confrontation.

I use this advice on a daily basis as a parent. I use it with staff and clients, too. It works because it eliminates the argument. This method takes confrontation completely out of the equation, because you can always bring your discussion back around to your initial agreement and the person cannot argue with what they already agreed to.

People like to know what's expected of them and how they can exceed your expectations. A good accountability plan details your expectations and provides a more positive environment and a better

Figure 3.1 – Keys to Systems, Measurement and Accountability

Obstacles	Benefits to Implementing Accountability
No point to accountability without measurement	Use tools available or create your own measurement tools!
Does not fit into "normal" business process	"DO" even if you don't know it all!
No one likes confrontation	Accountablity avoids confrontation

chance of your staff succeeding. Let me just describe this situation on the opposite side conversely. If you don't clearly define your expectations, you're leaving it up to your staff to define them. Naturally, they're going to determine the expectations by whatever is easiest for them to accomplish, right? Even worse, they might describe or define the expectations by their former employers' expectations.

Consider the consequences of using your competitors' employee expectations to run your business. These penalties are possible if you don't clearly define the expectations you have for your employees in your business.

Valuing Your Firm and Your Employees

As business owners, we need to constantly market our practice. We are marketing our business every day to prospective clients and employees. You need to not only market when you're hiring but continue to reinforce the value you bring to your staff by marketing the value of working at your firm.

Valuing your firm and your employees is extremely important. Periodically, taking a step back and examining your business from your employees' points of view will help you make improvements that can assist you in keeping your best team members for life.

It's a core tenet of the CTC™ philosophy that you must sell your value to your clients. Clients come to you for the numbers, and if you don't tell them how much you're worth, how else are they going to know? It's not enough to sell a value upfront, but you must consistently emphasize to your clients the value you bring from the money they invest in your services. Ask yourself why it wouldn't be just as important to sell the value of working with your firm to your employees. To put this into perspective, you may have up to several hundred clients. If you lose a client, it's not going to destroy your business. More than likely, you don't have hundreds of employees. If you lose an employee, or even worse, if you lose someone with top talent because you're not selling the value of working at your firm, it can essentially be a much greater loss than losing a client.

Determining an Employee's Value

I discussed in the first chapter of this book that you can determine the worth of potential employees by using the TALENT profile. Marketing the benefits you have to offer will not only help you attract the very best, it will assist in keeping this talent in your office, even if you can't afford the going rate for salary.

So how much is an employee really worth? I want to spend some time talking about the value of a good employee because it's helpful in developing your staffing budget and fundamental in making staffing decisions in your business.

I've developed a process to help you calculate the value of a good employee. It's far easier to calculate this value if you compare a good employee to the cost of a bad employee. Let's start by identifying some of the true costs of a bad employee. For example, consider the training cost lost from turnover and having to train a new member of your staff. I've illustrated an example for you in Figure 3.2. In my example, I use a staff member with an annual salary of $45,000 to perform the calculations. Naturally, you wouldn't have an increased training cost for a good employee, so I add $866 as a value to the "good employee" column.

We all know that bad employees cost additional time and productivity, either their own time or increased time for a new employee to get acquainted with the projects, assuming you have some turnover there, because you want to get rid of the bad.

In contrast, good employees will improve productivity as they become more and more familiar with the clients and with the workload, so I've added $9,006 in my example.

Bad employees can create dissatisfied clients who represent lost revenue once they take off and they can't stand it anymore. You'll see in my calculation, I took the average value of a client in the firm and multiplied it by the number of clients lost that a bad employee can cause you to lose.

Good employees will prevent lost clients and help retain revenues, so I've also added $5,000 in my example.

Good employees are also going to have a genuine interest in bringing in new business, especially if you incentivize them. Good

Figure 3.2

WHAT IS THE WORTH OF A Good Employee?

JOB OFFER CALCULATOR

JOB QUALITY				
	Bad/Lost Employee		Good Employee	
Training	# of hours x hourly rate	(866.00)	Maintain/leverage training	866.00
Productivity	Additional time for new EE hourly x rate	(9,006.00)	Increased productivity	9,006.00
Clients	Average value of clients x # of clients lost	(5,000.00)	Clients retained	5,000.00
Referrals	Average value of clients x # of clients gained	0.00	Average value of clients x # of clients gained	5,000.00
	TOTAL COST	($14,872)	TOTAL VALUE	$19,872

This calculation does not factor in the cost of lost opportunities, low staff morale, aggravation and staffing headaches. Use the checklist below to consider whether your current or potential employee is helping to create or to solve workplace problems. Check all that apply:

Bad/Lost Employee		Good Employee	
Opportunity for better employee lost		No additional hiring	
Costs boss time/aggravation		Creates freedom for boss	
Long-term problems in office		Solves office problems	
Discourages other staff		Encourages other staff	
Irritates clients		Pleases clients	
Other:		Other:	
TOTAL:		TOTAL:	

employees will refer new clients. In my example, let's assume a bad employee would not refer any business, represented by zeros in my example; while a good employee will refer business. I've added $5,000 to the value of a good employee.

This, of course, doesn't take into consideration the non-quantifiable costs of keeping a bad employee — things like aggravating other staff members, residual problems in the office, and client irritation should also be taken into account. These items are listed to acknowledge the non-cost and monetary benefits of good employees over bad ones.

And, on the flip side, you'll notice in my equation that the opposite is true of a good employee. A good employee creates freedom for their boss. The good employee solves office problems. A good employee encourages other staff and improves morale in the office and pleases clients. It's important to take into account the non-monetary costs, as well.

Last, it's really important to know the value of a good employee so you can approach a compensation package with an open mind and from a value perspective.

When you know how much it would cost you to get rid of a bad employee and try to replace him with a good employee, that information incentivizes you to create an attractive compensation package.

I'm not suggesting here that you look at the total value in my example and use that to make a compensation offer, but it's helpful to always have that in mind. Realizing the value of a good employee is also useful when an employee makes a special request. For instance, when you are approached by a staff member requesting an advance or special work arrangements, you are better prepared to answer their request if you understand the value your employee brings to your business.

Staff Accountability

Based on a recent AICTC™ poll, a staggering 72 percent of tax practitioners said they don't hold their staff accountable for performance. I'm sure tax business owners don't intend to be a part of that percentage, so this chapter focuses on how you can avoid this bad habit.

People like to know what is expected of them and how to exceed your expectations. So a good accountability plan outlines these details and provides a more positive environment and better chance of your team succeeding.

Make sure that your goals for your staff are primarily quantifiable. We all know there are some things you can't track or measure but you should aim for the majority of your staff's performance to be quantifiable and then make sure you measure it.

My suggestion here is to rate each and every project. Have you ever sat down to write a performance review and thought to yourself, "Now, what was it I wanted to make sure to remember at review time?" and you just can't quite put your finger on it. This goes back to the discussion about avoiding confrontation; if you are rating each and every project, you're now measuring it and you've got all the information you need to write a meaningful performance review. Your staff's performance will improve if they know that each and every project "counts."

A good accountability system provides consequences and rewards. This chapter is focused on incentives in order to retain good staff, but this really applies to clear communication of consequences, as well. It is the "carrot and the stick argument," which refers to the belief that offering a combination of rewards and punishments induces desired behaviors.

Performance Meetings

Another key to successful accountability is to have routine group performance meetings. It can be quite awkward to call a special meeting to talk about a problem, but if you have routine group performance meetings, you have a system in place for publically addressing the issues that come up, as well as praise for your staff.

Providing public reporting for your staff also improves their performance. Knowing their peers are watching and judging, employees are likely to work better to impress their coworkers. This also helps with process improvement. When you're discussing performances regularly, such as during weekly staff meetings, for example, you can get a more rapid response on the projects, and you can quickly identify obstacles that may be blocking performance. That may include your processes and systems. Getting this level of instant feedback enables you to adjust your processes and it improves your work system as a whole.

Performance Reviews

Consider conducting regular individual performance reviews. The term, "regular," however, is subjective. What might be regular for one practice may not benefit another. For example, an annual performance review isn't enough if you have clients who are calling and visiting every day of the year.

Performance reviews are a really great tool in going back to your original expectations, consequences, and rewards. These reviews are a vital part of the accountability system. You must consistently evaluate your staff's performance in relation to your expectations and key indicators for your business.

In chapter one, I shared with you a method to outline your TALENT profile. In that process, you identified desired results for your business and characteristics of your team to assist you in accomplishing those endeavors. Whatever your key indicators may be, it is essential to evaluate your employee's performance in correlation to your desired results.

You might consider rating your employees based on a set of core competencies. Some of the competencies you might consider in your tax business would be:

- Technical Knowledge;
- Productivity;
- Accuracy;
- Written and Oral Communications;
- Dependability;
- Innovation;
- Initiative;
- Problem Solving;
- Judgment;
- Planning and Organization;
- Attendance and Punctuality;
- Management Skills, and;
- Analytical Skills.

Ranking System

Once you've identified your own key indicators or core competencies, each one of your employees should be rated on a scale in each of the areas. I've used a rating scale of one to five in my practice. You can also apply additional measurements to assist you in the ranking.

As an example of how you can rank a category, under productivity, you may want to use your realization reports or measurement system for tracking realization on projects. Under accuracy, you may look at how many times returns have been reviewed. This is why measurement is such a vital part of the accountability process. You cannot hold someone accountable for something you aren't measuring. Implementing systems in your office to measure performance is a large part of the accountability process. Measurement will always be useful when assessing and improving your practice.

Self Reviews

The self review is an important tool that you can use in evaluating performance. It also causes the employee to reflect on each of the key areas of importance and acknowledge areas of weakness for improvement, as well as strength. Further, it's another way to clearly communicate your expectations.

The self review is also a chance for the employee to call attention to their accomplishments for you to use in developing their performance review. Basically, you want your staff to ask the question, "What have I done to increase revenues, productivity, and quality in our office?"

Self reviews build team mentality. As soon as your employees complete this task once, they'll go throughout the year remembering what is required of them to improve their performances. It's going to stick on their minds as they're going through each project.

Rewards and Consequences

Getting your staff to agree to consequences and rewards initially helps avoid confrontation when the going gets tough. For example,

CTC™ members use performance contracts as a perfect way to clearly communicate the expectations and the rewards for particular tasks. Performance contracts are signed agreements with your employees. They state every expectation upfront, which reduces conflict and confusion in the future.

Ask yourself, "Am I clearly communicating rewards and consequences to my staff on a regular basis?" If you answered, "No," develop a system to correct the lack of communication in your office.

Signed performance contracts should be used in collaboration with clearly communicating rewards and consequences. This enables a serious commitment from your staff in-writing that they not only understand your expectations, such as the consequences and the rewards, but they also are agreeing to the terms you have outlined for them in their job descriptions.

Compensation Packages

If you factor in other incentives and benefits that you may have to offer, you can really reduce your labor costs, while offering an attractive total compensation package. This section is really devoted to helping you uncover those hidden benefits that you didn't know were available to you.

This is where you can really stretch your labor budget. You may have benefits available that you need to consider and market them as the total compensation package.

Incentivizing staff can produce rewarding outcomes. Since you may not have an endless bank account, you can stretch your budget by using non-conventional compensation. This helps to retain your top talent as well.

Alternative Incentives

Let's discuss alternative benefits and incentives. The following are a few suggestions to consider when incentivizing your employees.

Flexible Hours and Telecommuting

Flexible scheduling is an attractive incentive to people in today's economy, especially when living in an area where traffic can add hours to someone's work schedule. The ability to work a flexible schedule can be deemed valuable by employees.

Consider stay-at-home parents. The ability to work from home when kids are home from school or to be able to work virtually at night when children are asleep is very valuable to many parents. It may be so valuable that they are willing to work for a lower wage in exchange for that particular benefit.

Fringe Benefits

How about providing a health club membership for your staff members? It may have a slight monthly fee attached, but it's something that your competitors aren't offering. You can get very creative with fringe benefits. You can consider theme park or natural park season passes, discount cards or entertainment membership programs. The point is to be able to present a unique and full-compensation or incentive package. Know your staff and what would appeal to them.

Strategic Alliances to Provide Services

I encourage my coaching clients to partner with complimentary professionals to help build their businesses. It may be applicable to reach out to your professional network to provide discounted services to your employees.

Usually, these benefits can provide valuable perks at little to no cost to your practice. Perhaps you partner with a financial planner or real estate professional. Can they provide a service to your staff, such as a financial plan or a no-cost loan? Weigh your options within your network. There may be several hidden assets that you can utilize.

Other Incentives

The AICTC™ conducted surveys of tax business owners and asked them about the incentives they use that really "wow" their staffs.

One of the most common benefits suggested was the ability to work from home. Other suggestions include giving employees a cash bonus for bringing in a new client. This benefits both parties; if you're looking to implement a new process in your office or bring in referrals, put together an incentive to drive it. If you want to change something, incentivize it, and that will get people moving on it.

Other examples we received was to provide an employee and his or her family with an all-expense-paid vacation or getaway. This is a higher-end incentive. Remember, incentives don't have to be extravagant. You can take your entire staff to a movie, have a luncheon, or even hold a company field trip. It's the memorable experience that will make employees say, "There's no other employer in town that takes the staff to the movies once a year." Your employees will appreciate your appreciating them.

Bonuses

Connecting performance to compensation as an incentive is a great way to save your labor budget and improve performance. When you use compensation as a performance incentive, you can drastically reduce your financial commitment to your staff. Consider offering your team a reduced wage-base offer. You can hold the difference aside as an available bonus pool. For example, if you have a staff member who would earn $30,000 annually, you may consider offering 10 to 15 percent less and setting that percentage aside as a bonus pool for that particular staff member. Based on performance, the difference in salary is awarded during a performance review.

Integrating Performance Reviews and Incentives

As mentioned earlier in this chapter, developing staff performance reviews is critical when running a tax business. Remember you're simply ranking each employee on a scale of one to five in each of your core competency areas. Once you've ranked the performance of your employees, then you can determine the incentives to reward accordingly.

One way to integrate performance-based incentives is by awarding a portion of an available bonus pool based on a performance review score. Let's say that you're ranking your employees on a scale of one to five and you average out the total score, which as an example, I'll say is 3.25. Next, express that average as a percentage. Take 3.25 and divide it by five, which is the total possible score. Once you convert their score into a percentage, multiply that percentage against the bonus pool. The formula in my example is one way to calculate an employee bonus based on performance. A benefit of this method is that it is simple enough for your staff to understand the calculation, which motivates them to perform well.

One thing is for sure: employees enjoy bonuses. They're also happy because they see room for improvement. In each and every performance review, use that time to communicate with staff to develop goals for improvement. Once someone has experienced more than one performance review, rescore them based on their own performance goals they set for themselves. This method has been very successful with tax business owners who have implemented it in their own practices across the country.

In a recent AICTC™ poll, we asked tax business owners if they've tied their employees' compensation incentives with their performance reviews, and about half of those polled answered, "No." If you haven't already begun associating performance reviews with staff incentives, do so as soon as possible.

As an added benefit to your tax practice, connecting your staff member's performance reviews to their compensation incentives is a great way to decrease your staffing budget and attract top talent.

Common Traps

- **Having accountability without measurement.**
  There is really no point to having accountability without measurement. I hope that you'll use the tools I've shared with you to help you measure your staff's performance and key factors in your business.

When you hold your staff accountable for their performance, you incentivize them to perform better, which you can recognize through measurement. A diagram of this is provided in Figure 3.3.

As you can see, you can't have accountability without measurement, and you can't have measurement without accountability.

- **Not doing everything you can to avoid confrontation.**
  We mentioned before that signed performance contracts are an ideal way to avoid future conflict. One CTC™ member illustrated this point with a personal experience:

  "I had a staff member once for a year that just wasn't cutting the mustard. She just wasn't going to make it. I used accountability systems, so that part was easy. I was measuring her performance and all the writing was on the wall that it just didn't seem like this person was going to work out, but what I didn't do was have routine meetings, including performance feedback. At that time, I was doing a once-a-year performance review.
  I have to tell you, there's nothing worse than suddenly asking a staff member to come into your office and close the door behind you. It's awkward. They know it. The whole staff listening outside the door with glasses pressed against the wall – they know it. I called her into my office and spent an hour firing her. Of course, she exited the office with red, puffy eyes and everyone knew something bad had just happened. She gathered her things, and she left right away."

  No one wants to experience awkward situations in the workplace. By setting guidelines beforehand, you'll do yourself and your employees a favor, highlighting expectations and evading confrontation.

  With signed performance contracts, you're no longer susceptible to argument over what the person agreed to do, because you got that buy-in; you get that agreement upfront before there's a conflict.

  Furthermore, you could always bring the argument back around to what they initially agreed to do. Then, when that person fails to do it, you have predesigned consequences, and again, there's no confrontation.

Figure 3.3 – Accountability through Measurement and Incentivizing

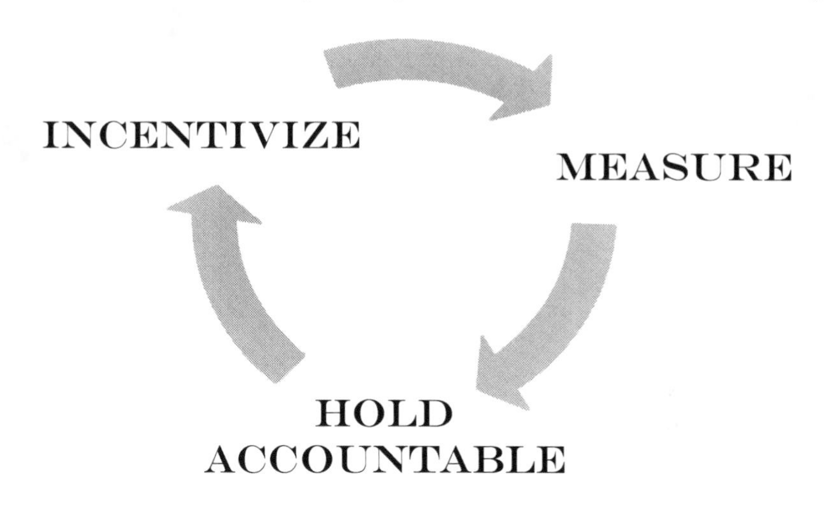

Frequently Asked Questions

- **Would CTC™ consider paying for employees' Continuing Professional Education (CPE) costs each year as a viable fringe benefit acceptable?**
  Absolutely, and if you're currently paying for CPE or if you're doing in-house CPE, you need to make sure that you're quantifying that and you're reminding your staff of the value. Investing in their education is a perfect way to see improvement from and get additional value out of your employees, as well. You're going to have better staff members because of it.

- **I'm considering giving staff a set percentage of the fees on their completed work in lieu of an hourly wage. Would you recommend this?**
  It's a core CTC™ principle that hourly billing is a lousy way to make a living. You are billing for your services according to the effort or time that goes into them and that has no relationship to the value of the service that you are providing the client. Well, if you accept the philosophy of moving away from hourly billing to the clients, why, then, would you not reconsider the value of hourly billing from

your employee to you? That's essentially what your employee is doing when you pay him or her on an hourly basis. The employee is billing you hourly for their time without a guaranteed relationship to the value of that time. Paying staff members based on commission removes that disconnect between you and your employees. It puts you and your employee both on the same side looking to maximize revenue and productivity for the firm.

- **How do you transition from fixed annual salary to pay based on performance? How do you reset a regular pay in the near term?**
  You may think that would reduce pay, but you may be surprised. Employees may end up earning more, and if you're earning more as a result of their efforts, you should consider a very thorough total compensation package. Try to highlight the benefits of it from the employee's point of view. For example, if it's going to give the employees more flexibility with their schedule or the freedom to do projects the way they want to, highlight those benefits. Even include new benefits in the new package. Some of the benefits that we went over earlier in this chapter may spice it up and give the feeling of a full compensation package.

- **What is the best system you found to share QuickBooks with virtual support staff? Do you provide your employees with remote access to your servers?**
  I recommend virtual private networking that can be done through hardware and software, but you should also consider software solutions available for cloud computing. In cloud computing, your data is stored on a hosted, remote server. It's also a great way to do that with clients so that both you and your clients can log into their QuickBooks file. You can even be on the network simultaneously if you have multiple licenses.

  It's also convenient because it provides one common area for files, important records, and documents and communication you can use to send messages back and forth. There are tools out there available on the market. They have online versions, and they have

Figure 3.4

KEYS TO A SUCCESSFUL

Accountability System

- Provide employees with clear expectations.
- Ensure that goals are primarily quantifiable.
- Develop your accountability plan in advance.
- Provide consequences and rewards.
- Require signed performance contracts.
- Conduct regular, routine performance meetings.

the ability to access the files remotely.

- **How can a bonus package be put together when an eight-hour day does not have eight hours of billable time?**

  The quick answer to that is get away from billable hours on the part of clients and the part of staff. It's basic productivity.

  Also, it refers back to the concept of paying for performance. I think when you pay based on performance, even with a bonus structure, you are getting away from the hourly pay method, and that's what I encourage tax business owners to do.

  It's really the only way that you can increase your realization, because when you're tied to hourly billing, it's a limited resource. There's only 24 hours in a day, and there's only so much "that the industry will bear for going rates," which has been proven to be nonexistent anyways, but it's people's perception of the going rate. When you can charge on a flat-fee basis, you really can be making thousands of dollars per hour.

- **Is it pretty common to pay the employee portion of health insurance?**
  Health insurance is getting to be a very expensive benefit to offer. There are several people in the tax industry that are not currently offering that benefit. Look for ways that you can stretch your dollar. Before you commit to this, make sure it's justifiable to pay the employee portion of health insurance or for full-family coverage, which is often considered more than generous.

- **How can you ensure that your employees who "work from home" are really working?**
  One of the things that employers are hesitant about when it comes to flextime and working from home is, "Am I really going to be paying my staff this professional hourly rate to get work done, or are they going to spend half of their time on Facebook?" and if you can divorce the compensation from the time it takes to do the work, you eliminate that worry entirely. Plus, you give the employee the incentive to focus on productivity. I mentioned before how you want to sell the value of working for your firm to your employees, just as you want to sell the value of being a client to your clients. You are able to do that with certain benefits like the ability to telecommute.

  When you pay based on performance, even with a bonus structure, you are getting away from the hourly pay method, which eliminates the possibility that you are paying your employee for non-work time.

DID YOU KNOW?

"Having an operations manual and well-documented system for running things demonstrates that the business can be maintained profitable after sale and will enhance business value."[3]

Chapter Three in Review

This chapter addressed the importance of accountability systems in your tax practice.

How can accountability systems benefit your practice? Accountability systems:

- Can be the most effective employee and supervisory tracking method when properly coupled with measurement;
- Can be of great assistance in assessing staff performance, which assists the hiring, managing, and firing processes, and;
- Can eliminate confrontation by expressing expected behaviors, predesigned consequences, and possible rewards.

In order to genuinely value your employees, you must determine their values. This chapter provided an example of how a good employee can save you money, whereas a bad employee could cost you hundreds, if not thousands, of dollars annually.

Your employees will appreciate knowing what is expected of them and how to exceed your expectations. Superior accountability plans outline these details and provide a more positive environment and the high probability of your team succeeding.

There are several ways you can employ accountability, including:

- **Performance Meetings.** Public reporting to your staff can improve their performance.
- **Performance Reviews.** Regularly schedule meetings with your staff to address expectations, consequences, and rewards. Although, note that "regular" performance reviews apply differently to every separate tax practice according to its particular needs. Base your reviews on the following 13 core competencies:

  Technical Knowledge;
  Productivity;

Accuracy;
Written and Oral Communications;
Dependability;
Innovation;
Initiative;
Problem Solving;
Judgment;
Planning and Organization;
Attendance and Punctuality;
Management Skills, and;
Analytical Skills.

- **Ranking System.** Rank each one of your employees from one to five, based on the core competencies you recognize as important to your practice.
- **Self Reviews.** Self reviews allow employees to reflect on their strengths and weaknesses in order to continue achievement and/or to improve upon flaws.
- **Rewards and Consequences.** Signed performance contracts should be used in collaboration with clearly communicating rewards and consequences.
- **Compensation Packages.** Incentivizing staff builds employee morale and helps retain top talent at your firm.

Your employees will appreciate the effort you give into reviewing their performances and rewarding them when applicable. Having both accountability and measurement systems, never one without the other, can greatly improve performance in your office.

CHAPTER FOUR

Minimizing Liabilities in Your Tax Business

With the constant changes in law, interpretations in the law, and case law, it's vital that as tax business owners, we keep up-to-date to maintain our liabilities at a minimum. While the constant changes and breadth of the laws make it impossible to identify each employer requirement, this chapter will introduce you to the major areas of potential employment liability and help you identify when you need to consult an employment law professional.

According to a recent AICTC™ poll, only 38 percent of polled tax business owners have a plan to minimize liability risk in their tax practices. About two-thirds of those asked are at-risk of some kind of tax liability, which is very dangerous when operating a tax business.

This chapter is extremely important, because most employers, especially when dealing with small businesses, are so busy taking care of their clients and figuring out how to minimize risks for their clients, that they don't take the necessary time to make sure that they're running their businesses in a way that minimizes their own personal liability.

Paying Your Employees

A lot of tax business owners will admit that they fail to stay current on hourly and salary wage laws. In fact, only eight percent of polled tax practitioners consult with attorneys. I would like to provide some value to you to point out specific areas perhaps you're unfamiliar with. This information is intended to help educate you to recognize things that you can do to protect your business.

Employment laws change constantly. They don't only change in the statutory context, but current legal cases occurring may be relied upon by the courts, and these are not cases of mass interest that your local media is going to cover. The only way to really stay on top of the changes is to have an attorney who's either sending you updates or that you can call and consult with regularly. It's beneficial to have a relationship with a professional who's going to be on top of the recent cases and new laws.

Properly Classifying Employees

According to recent statistics published by the Department of Labor, over 70% of business are not compliant with the Fair Labor Standards Act, which is the federal law that governs how employees must be paid. This area of employment law can be confusing for business owners to understand. The wage and hour aspects of employment law, and more specifically determining whether your employee is hourly or salary, can have significant consequences in determining whether a business is properly paying its employees.

There are three ways to classify the people who work for you. First, there are independent contractors, who are different from an employee, because you don't have to pay employer payroll taxes for independent contractors. There are other benefits, such as not having to pay Worker's Compensation for them. Additional benefits vary by state. In the state of California, there's a disability fund that employers pay into only if the people working for them are employees, which is another advantage of being able to classify those who work for you as independent contractors. While classifying those who work for you as independent contractors is generally fiscally advantageous, misclassification can leave your company liable for back wages, back taxes, and penalties which often exceed actual liability. Be sure to consult with a professional to ensure proper classification of your employees. The key question to ask when deciding whether to classify someone as an independent contractor is: Are they really independent? Do they bear their own risk of loss, run their own payroll, run their own business, set their own hours, and have the discretion and independent judgment that comes with being independent? If the answer is "no," the conservative course of action is to hire them as employees.

There are also exempt employees and non-exempt employees. Let's first distinguish between exempt employees and non-exempt ones. A non-exempt employee is a regular hourly worker, while an exempt employee signifies that they are exempt from federal and state wage and hour laws. The federal Fair Labor Standards Act governs every employee in every state who is an hourly employee and who is non-exempt.

Each state is also allowed to enact their own wage and hour laws, so when evaluating the requirements of the federal wage and hour laws, you should bear in mind that your state may go above and beyond those federal requirements, especially in states like California. California tends to be the most employee-friendly state. Please be aware that this chapter is covering federal laws, and your state may be more stringent.

Non-exempt employees are hourly employees. On the other hand, exempt employees are a group of employees that are not subject to the Fair Labor Standards Act wage and hour state laws, and generally in business are referred to as "salary" employees.

The exemptions to the Fair Labor Standards Act each have specific requirements, each of which must be met to qualify for the exemption. In addition, each of the exemptions are construed narrowly by the courts. The failure to comply with each requirement of the applicable exemption could result in a court finding that your salary employees are really hourly employees, holding you liable for back-wages, overtime, penalties, and the employee's attorneys' fees.

One of the key requirements of each exemption is to determine whether the duties the employee is performing are exempt of non-exempt duties. Federal law looks to what the employee's "primary" duties are. In a qualitative sense, primary duty is defined as an employee's role within the company. Is a person there because he or she is supposed to be managing, or is he or she there because they're supposed to be doing secretarial tasks?

Depending on its employment laws, your state could analyze the primary duty quantitatively, meaning for 51 percent of the employee's time, are they doing exempt or non-exempt tasks? For example, California and other similar states do not measure the primary duty, but instead look at duties quantitatively, meaning, what is the employee actually doing for the majority (51%) of his or her time at work? These cases are very fact driven and as an employer, you may find yourself in a factual battle with your employee regarding how many minutes of each day are spent performing each task. As precautionary measure, you do want to be aware of the differences between your state's law and the federal law in that aspect and seek consultation from a professional to implement appropriate company policies to protect you.

There are several major exempt employee areas. You should pay close attention to each of these requirements when you are ready to hire.

Executive Exemption

The first major exempt employee area is called the executive exemption. For the executive exemption, the requirements are as follows.

- **Your executive exempt employee must have a salary rate of at least $455 a week.** There is a quantitative salary requirement for executive exemption. The employee must earn the same salary every week. Paying your employee less than either the federal or state minimum, or less than agreed could result in your exempt employee losing his or her exemption.
- **The executive exempt employee's primary duty must be management of the enterprise or management of a customarily recognized department or subdivision thereof.** More simply, this means that the employee is either managing your entire business, or they're managing a distinct division of your business.

- **The employee must customarily and regularly direct the work of two or more other employees**. The executive exemption is designed to target your employees that are managing either the entire company or a portion of that company and are directly managing other people. Many cases exist where business owners try to classify their employees under this exemption, and when asked how many people they are directing, they are really only directing themselves. This is a big requirement and is typically one that is most frequently failed.
- **The employee is given authority.** The employee must have the authority to hire or fire other employees or his or her suggestions and recommendations as to the hiring, firing, advancement, promotion or any other change of status of other employees are given particular weight.

Administrative Exemption

Another area of employee exemption is the administrative exemption. The requirements for the administrative exemption are as follows.

- **Your administrative exempt employee must have a salary rate of at least $455 a week.** This is the same requirement as the executive exempt employees.
- **The primary duty is the performance of office or non-manual work directly related to management or general business operations.** As with executive exemption, administrative exemption dictates the type and manner of work employees under this designation should be performing.
- **The primary duty includes the exercise of discretion and independent judgment with respect to matters of significance**. This third and final requirement is typically the most problematic for employers. The most important distinction to make when considering this requirement is the amount of leeway the employee is given to use their discretion and independent judgment with respect to matters of significance. You will want to be careful with the administrative exemption. It is the exemption with the biggest amount of interpretation built into the requirements, and it is the exemption that is subject to the

most litigation and investigations by the Department of Labor.

If you are considering giving an employee an administrative exemption, first ask yourself the following questions.

- **Does this person truly have the ability to exercise free judgment and discretion with consideration to important business matters?**
- **Do you give direction regarding the execution of this person's duties?**
- **With important decisions, does this person come back to you for guidance?**
- **Is this person really an administrative assistant or secretary? Do not be fooled by the title of the exemption; it does not apply to administrative assistants.**

Learned Professional Exemption

A third area of exemption is the "Learned Professional Exemption." The requirements are as follows.

- **The learned professional exempt employee must be performing work that requires advanced knowledge.** Advanced knowledge means that the knowledge you have and the knowledge you've gained is such that you're required to use it in a manner that uses your independent discretion and judgment. Thus, we're again going back to the independent judgment and use of discretion factor, which really means you know what you do, it took a long time to learn it, you are specialized in your field, you're someone within your organization who has an area of knowledge that not everyone else has, so you're really required to use your learning and your judgment to do your job correctly.
- **The learned professional exempt employee works in a field of recognized science or learning.**
- **The learned professional exempt employee works in an industry that customarily requires prolonged courses of specialized intellectual instruction.**

Other Exemptions

There are exemptions for computer professionals, creative professionals, teachers, outside sales people, and highly paid people, and that means that they're making in excess of $100,000 a year.

Special Employment Law Definitions

Minimum Wage

There are minimum wages, and there are different minimum wages in the federal law context and the state law context. Again, under the Fair Labor Standards Act, the minimum wage is the absolute minimum, so states are permitted to enact legislation that increases the federal minimum wage. Under federal law, overtime must be paid after 40 hours of work per week. Certain states also have provisions for daily overtime and for overtime at a rate of twice the employee's regular rate of pay.

Work Week Definition

A work week is seven consecutive days; however, it does not have to start on a Monday. An employer is allowed to set his or her own work week. It can begin on Monday at 8 AM; it can start on Wednesday in the afternoon. Nonetheless, how you want to set your work week is at your full discretion as the employer. Once you set it, it is your work week. It is very difficult to change. There are circumstances under which you can change it in the future, but it it's very difficult to show that you're changing it for a justifiable reason as opposed to changing it to in some way avoid paying the overtime you're currently paying.

Basically, the rule of thumb is if you're saving money by changing your work week, you're probably doing something that violates the law. Think hard about when you want your work week to begin and end before setting it permanently.

Work Day Definition

Work days are defined similarly to work weeks. A work day is a 24-hour period, but that workday can be set by the employer. The employer can start a work day at 8 AM or at midnight. Depending on how you set your workday, if you're in a state like California, where there are daily overtime provisions, it will make a big difference in terms of how much you're paying your employees for overtime.

For example, a company that uses an 8 AM start time for its workday is going to pay a lot more overtime if it's has people who are working the night shift because that shift wraps around to the next morning. Account for time at the end of the day's laws at the beginning of the day, because once you set your workday, it's an undeviating, consecutive 24-hour period.

Work Hour Definition

You may have employees that start at 9:00 in the morning, but every morning they come in at 8:30 AM, and you allow it, because they claim to be surfing the internet and conducting non-work-related activities. However, they're actually getting a jumpstart on the day; maybe they're checking emails or organizing their schedules. Even if you tell them not to perform a single second of work until 9 AM, if they're present at 8:30, you need include that time in their pay hours. Working time is all time that's permitted to work or "suffered" to work. "Suffering work" means that if you're employee is actually at work, if they're permitted to work, even if they're not required to do so and if you are creating circumstances that allow them to work, you need to pay that employee for the time that they're working.

Donning and Doffing

There are also circumstances under which you have to pay your employees before they're working. This is called "donning and doffing," and that literally means putting on and taking off. So if you have a uniform or some sort of specialized attire or adornment that the employee has to put on his or her person, workspace, car, etc., there is a chance that you will have to be paying your employee to do those activities.

On-Call Time

There are circumstances when you have to pay your employee to be on-call, even if your employee is at home sleeping. Factors that are taken into consideration are: one, the degree in which the employee is free to engage in personal activity, and two, any agreements between the parties.

Generally, if the employee is allowed to be at home to eat with his family, to sleep in his own bed, to go an hour away to a party, whatever the case may be, you don't have to pay them for that time. If the employee is allowed to be at home but is required to answer his home phone or is required to answer the phone call and to report to duty dressed within 10 minutes, then you're really not giving that person enough room to do what they would otherwise do with free time, so under those circumstances, you would have to pay your employee for on-call time.

Regular Rate of Pay

The current overtime rate stands at 1.5 times the regular rate of pay. What is the regular rate of pay? If your answer is, "Whatever the hourly rate is," you're wrong and you could be subject to liability. The regular rate of pay is more than just the hourly wage; it includes all compensation other than benefits. For example, if you also pay your employee in goods or services, you need to include the value of those goods and services into your regular rate of pay.

If you pay your employees a bonus, that bonus could very well be included in your regular rate of pay. The types of bonuses that are included are bonuses that are set by contract in terms of amount or eligibility, where there is no discretion by the employer. For instance, if every year at your employee's year anniversary, you give a bonus of $1,000, that $1,000 needs to be taken into account when you're determining the regular rate of pay for overtime, and the way that you do that is if you're giving a $1,000 a year bonus, you divide that $1,000 into the number of pay periods, and for each pay period, you add whatever that fraction is to the number of hours that are worked in that pay period. Rather than $10 an hour, you'll calculate a total, such as $10.25 an hour. Be aware that when you're paying overtime or setting your overtime rates, you do need to account for bonuses.

The only bonus you will not have to take into account when setting your regular rate is the bonus not promised to the employee. Bonuses are considered discretionary, if there is a question whether you pay it and the amount you pay. If, for example, you have a bonus that's given to employees who do a good job, it's entirely discretionary to the employer to determine whether the employee does a good job. On the other hand, if the employee meets certain specified goals that constitute a "good job," they're entitled to a $5,000 bonus, and that amount is set in stone, the amount is not discretionary. Likely, that's a bonus that you're going to have to factor into the regular rate of pay.

Commissioned Employees

There are other types of employees, like commission employees. It's a little more difficult to determine what an hourly rate is for these employees, and they're not paid like hourly employees. They're not given $10 an hour; they're paid based on what they sell or the services that they provide or the income that comes into the company. Commission employees are acceptable under the Fair Labor Standards Act.

The one thing that you'll have to watch out for is just to make sure that those commission employees are always earning the minimum wage. The statute seems to allow a commission employee to make $20,000 in one month and zero the next month. Also, it says if there's any overflow, or any overage of the minimum wage that was made in one month; the overage can be carried over into the next month. This is good news, but be aware that there are federal cases that have come down since that statute has been enacted that seemed to reverse that language. The best course of action is to make sure your commissioned employees are always earning at least the minimum wage.

Break Periods

The last two brief, yet broader topics are rest periods and meal periods. If your employees are taking short rest periods of five to even up to 20 minutes to get a snack, get a cup of coffee, go to the restroom, this type of time is considered on-duty and you need to pay them for it. On the contrary, meal periods are different. If an employee is given a meal period where they are not working and that period of time is at least 30 minutes, you do not have to pay for that time. In most states, meal and rest periods are mandatory, and if you don't comply with them, you could be issued a financial penalty.

How Employment Law Applies to Tax Professionals

There are instances in the tax industry where an administrative staff member might be paid a salary based on 2,080 hours a year. This is kind of a unique situation for tax professionals, who outside of tax season might work 30-35 hours a week, but during tax season, or the weeks between January and April, they work about 45 hours a week. There are times like these when tax practices offer alternative work schedules to their employees.

Please note that the federal law does not provide for alternative work week schedules, so you will have to look at your individual state's law. There may be some exceptions to the rule, but the federal law does not provide for an exception other than collective bargaining agreements, so again, confirm your state's laws regarding this matter.

Non-Compete Agreements

Some states' courts do not hesitate to deny non-compete agreements. A non-compete agreement must be narrowly tailored in terms of the scope of the non-compete agreement as well as the geographic scope and the length of time.

The big issue is a lot of these non-compete agreements try to prevent the employee from using the scope that the employer has gained over the course of 20 years and prevent them for using them for a competing company. This is difficult to overcome. This is especially true in strict states, where the state is extremely protective over its citizens' ability to practice their professions.

If you have a non-compete agreement, have an attorney review it, because if it's not narrowly drafted, it can be voided entirely.

Discrimination

Discrimination is a concern at every stage of employment: at hiring, when you're promoting people, when you're giving bonuses, when you're giving preferences in assignments, and when you're terminating. You have to ask yourself at each stage, "Why am I doing this? Am I doing something that I could subject me to liability later on?"

The types of discrimination that are protected by the federal law under Title 7 are race, color, ethnicity, disability, age, religion, and gender, which include issues such as pregnancy and/or marital status. For example, in a situation where applicants who are women with young children are not hired, but men with young children are hired, bias of familial status could turn into a strong gender discrimination case.

Another area of discrimination is disability. Disability can be tricky, because there are things that may impact a hiring decision that could or could not be related to disability. If you are going to take that into consideration when hiring, you better be accurate that your decision is not related to a disability. Factors, such as obesity, alcoholism, contagious disease, and of course something like diabetes or the need to take frequent breaks to test blood sugar levels, could all be classified as disability discrimination if handled improperly.

There's also age discrimination, which covers people over 40 years old, and religious discrimination. "Religion" doesn't refer to any particular established religion; it covers any belief that sincerely helps as though it was a religion. This is a gray area, but some courts have said that even a strongly held refusal to have a belief is a belief that can be subjected to religious discrimination.

Attention deficit disorder can also be considered a disability. As an employer, this is something you don't need to be aware of in order to manage employees. On the topic of discrimination, what you *don't know* can't come back to haunt you. The only question you need answered is, "Can you perform the essential functions of the job with or without reasonable accommodation?" If someone has no disabilities, they'll answer, "Yes." If someone has a disability and a reasonable accommodation would allow them to perform their job, then they'll also answer, "Yes."

When it comes to reasonable accommodation, once an employee discloses a disability or a need for a reasonable accommodation, you have an affirmative duty to have a discussion with that employee about whether there are any reasonable accommodations the company can provide to allow that employee to continue to work or to work more comfortably. If there are, you must provide a reasonable accommodation, which does not necessarily have to be the accommodation the employee requested.

Sexual Harassment

The laws are not designed to create a completely sterile environment. We are all people; it's in our nature to have platonic relationships with the people we work with. We see them for many hours a day. We care about them as people, and it's natural when someone we interact with all the time feels badly about themselves and you want to give them a compliment to boost their self esteem.

Just be careful. Choose your words and select your times very carefully. Remember, if it's something that you wouldn't say to your mom, then you probably shouldn't say it to your employee. For example, someone coming in and saying to a woman, "You look very nice today." On the occasional, appropriate basis, it's not going to cause the reasonable person to feel uncomfortable, but hearing it every day might, so just take that into consideration.

If an employee complains to you or another manager that he or she has been subject to sexual harassment, you as the employer have an affirmative duty to do what you can to prevent it, this usually includes conducting an investigation and if necessary, disciplining or terminating anyone found to have harassed an employee.

Quid Pro Quo

One type of sexual harassment is quid pro quo, which translates as "this for that." This occurs when an authoritative figure exchanges sexual favors with an associate, such as a promotion or vacation pay. This is of course illegal and creates legal liability for the business owner engaging in this type of behavior.

Hostile Work Environment

The second type of sexual harassment is a hostile work environment. The hostile work environment claim means that you created a work environment that was so subject to sexual innuendo that it was uncomfortable for someone working there. For the particular employee who filed the claim, it was so bad that he or she could not perform work reasonably.

The one thing you want to be careful about in terms of hostile work environment is that a hostile work environment can be proven by an accumulation of a number of things. It doesn't have to be one major thing. It doesn't have to be pornographic material on the computer or really crass jokes about the individual. It could be more subtle things, such as off-colored remarks. They may not be overtly offensive comments, but someone might take offense to them.

Assess your environment and ensure that even though you may not be doing anything explicitly sexual, there may be subtleties in your environment that could be put all together by a potential plaintiff when claiming a hostile work environment.

Terminating Employees

The first thing you should do when deciding to terminate an employee is ask yourself, "Are we going to have a problem here? Could we have a problem here?" If you find that you may be dealing with someone who's got a claim for liability, it may be a good idea to offer that person a severance in exchange for release of liability.

Most employees are at-will employees, meaning you can fire them for any reason or no reason at all, as long as it's not a discriminatory or sexual harassment-based reason. For most employees, you do not have to pay severance, you do not have to give notice, and if you're dealing with an at-will employee for whom you are going to terminate, you want to get a release of liability in exchange for some reasonable amount of severance. For hourly employees, a typical severance might be a week or two.

You also want to end the professional relationship at that time. You don't want to open yourself up to having an employee there who's going to be there for two weeks, who's disgruntled, who has access to your clients and your trade secrets, etc.

At-Will Employees

If an employee is at-will, you don't have to give any notice prior to terminating their employment with your practice. You can terminate an at-will reason for any reason or no reason, so long as it's not a illegal (discrimination or retaliation) reason. Probably, if you're terminating this person, it's because they didn't fit well with your business. You don't want anyone disgruntled to harm you later.

In most cases, you will want the freedom and flexibility of an at-will employment relationship. If you've hired people before, you know that you don't really know them until they've been working for you for a while. You don't want to be stuck in a situation where there's six months left on a person's contract, and you're just now figuring out at month three that their working habits are incompatible with your business.

Contract Employees

If the person you intend to terminate is not an at-will employee, he or she is probably a contract employee, and you're going to have to go back and look at the contract before you make a final decision. If you have a contract with an employee that provides for a specific amount of notice, you have to make sure you give that notice. If you have a contract with an employee for a one-year term of employment, and you're at the eight-month period and you want to end the relationship, you can do it, but you are in breach of the contract and could be responsible for the remaining four months of pay.

An oral contract constitutes a valid contract, so you have to be careful of what promises you make, too. Something as simple as saying, "Look, as long as you do a good job, you have a place with us," can be defined as a contract for employment. It doesn't have a specified term, but you've taken yourself out of the at-will arena. You've now created a situation where you can only fire this person if they're doing a bad job, and not just if they're doing a bad job, but if you can prove to a jury that they've done a bad job.

Again, you want to be careful and ensure that you adequately documented performance reviews that actually reflect the work that has been going on.

Documentation

If you're going to terminate for cause, in other words, for performance deficiencies, you want to have properly documented in that person's performance file that there were problems, that you made the person aware of the problems, and you gave them a reasonable opportunity to fix those problems. It's a good idea to launch three attempts to get the employee to do what they're supposed to be doing. Ideally, you're going to give a written counseling to employees about performance issues. If the problem persists, you will give another written warning, and this is the final written warning. If they still fail to improve, you'll plan to terminate for-cause.

Just be aware that termination doesn't happen overnight. You're going to want to make sure that you have enough time with the employee to lay the proper groundwork in their personnel file. You need to be able to prove that you told them what the problem was and you gave them opportunities to improve.

The periodic performance evaluation can be a very valuable tool in terms of documenting performance. However, many employers do not like to give bad feedback and as a result, all performance evaluations do not provide much information about the employee and do not identify the employee's deficiencies. If you are going to give performance evaluations, be honest. Honest feedback gives the employee the chance to improve and if the employee does not improve, gives you the documentation necessary to justify a for-cause termination.

Common Traps

- **Asking questions, such as, "Are we going to promote a woman to partner?"**
  A question specifically asked about gender can land you in hot water. Gender should not influence the decision-making process in your practice. If you're willing to talk about the sex of an employee, you better have a valid reason to do so. Keep in mind that when you're making hiring or promotion decisions, the person you're talking about has no defined gender. Otherwise, it could be quite easy to bring a gender discrimination claim against your firm.

- **Giving compliments that cross the line.**
  While it's perfectly fine to say in moderation, "You look very pretty today," "Wow, that dress is hot," is inappropriate and unacceptable. Only use conservative commentary in the workplace, or else you may be liable for a sexual harassment claim. An employee may not tell you if what you said made him or her uncomfortable. Remember, you are the boss and most employees will desire to please you. So the best course of action is to assume your employees are reasonable sensitive and conservative.

- **Thinking that no one from work views your social media page or blog.**
  Recently, social media websites, such as Facebook and Myspace, have become a major method of communication between peers. You might post a link or picture only intended for your friends, but someone from work might find it obscene. Also, public comments about the workplace and/or your employees are fair game. Be careful who you befriend on social media websites and confirm your privacy settings. An infraction on Facebook could actually lead to a harassment or discrimination claim against you.

Frequently Asked Questions

- **If you're a small business with only two employees, is it possible to have an employee that meets the executive exemption by managing the only other staff member in the office?**
  No, it's not. These are hard and fast requirements, and if an employee is not managing two or more employees, then he or she is not managing people in the capacity that is contemplated by this exemption.

- **What if someone manages a number of independent contractor relationships rather than employees? Will that allow someone to qualify under the executive exemption?**
  Unfortunately, no, it will not. Only employees are exempt in this case, and the reason for that is that the law really looks at

independent contractors like they are a completely separate business. For example, if you have someone who does all of the company's purchasing, they're, in effect, managing separate businesses. They're telling the separate business what they want. They're making sure the separate business complies and gives them what they're ordering.

In terms of the law, there's not much of a distinction between a purchaser and a manager of independent contractors. So, you do want to make sure that they are managing within your organization.

- **Are tax professionals considered creative professionals?**
  Tax professionals would not likely be considered creative professionals. The creative professionals exemption is intended to distinguish between work that primarily requires invention, imagination, originality, or talent – like the arts – and work that primarily depends on intelligence, diligence and accuracy. However, because of the area that we are practicing in is something that requires advanced learning and we need a degree for what we do, tax professionals are considered learned professionals.

- **What does it mean when we say that a person is exempt?**
  This means that a person is exempt from the federal wage and hour laws.

- **What happens if you instruct your employees or direct your employees to take these rest periods or meal periods and they don't do it? Who's responsible for this?**
  Under present-day federal law, it doesn't matter who's responsible, because time periods aren't mandatory, but your state may require mandatory breaks, which you'll have to comply with. In California, for example, you have to give your employee 10 minutes of paid break time for every four hours of work. Plus, you have to give your employee at least a half an hour of unpaid lunch breaks for every five hours of work that are performed.

- **Can an employee legally replace their allotted 10-minute per day rest period with downtime during the day?"**

If this person is not taking a formal 10-minute break, however, for at least 10 minutes in a four-hour period, he or she is experiencing "downtime," it's more than likely within legal parameters. That person could be on a personal phone call, searching the internet, out walking to Starbucks to get a cup of coffee, etc. All of those activities will constitute a 10-minute rest break.

- **Does an hourly employee have to fill-out a time card, or is it enough to say he or she worked eight hours a day?**
  All employees should fill-out a time card. Depending on what state you're in, it may or may not be an actual requirement, but the reason you want them to fill-out the time card is because if you accidentally misclassify an employee, and they're putting in eight hours a day, there's going to be a question of fact as to how long they were actually working. Instead of saying that they were working eight hours a day for 40 hours a week, what they're going to say is, "I was told to put in eight hours a day, so I did what I was told, but in actuality, I was working 10 hours a day, because every day when I left the office, I took work home with me. I was under the impression that I couldn't put that on my timecard." Then you'll have to back-pay the employee, as well as pay penalties, which can really add up. You want to do everything that you can to remove that question of fact later on with regards to how many hours were worked or whether a break was taken.

- **Does the employee have an obligation to notify you as an employer about a disability from which he or she suffers?**
  Yes and no. If the employee doesn't notify you and you don't know about the disability, then that employee's just not going to get a reasonable accommodation and cannot later sue you for failing to provide it or for discriminating on the basis of a disability of which you were unaware.

  It is the employee's obligation to let you know if there's a disability and they want a reasonable accommodation for it. If you don't know, there's nothing you can do about it, and the law affords no liability in those circumstances.

- **Does general liability insurance protect one from employee lawsuits?**
  Generally, no. There is a special kind of insurance called EPLI; it's Employment Practices Liability Insurance. That's the insurance you need if you want to be protected from discrimination, sexual harassment, and wage and hour lawsuits.

- **Are non-compete agreements upheld if you're just trying to restrict soliciting your clients?**
  Non-solicitation agreements, rather than non-compete agreements, will be upheld in most states as long as it's reasonably tailored in scope, time and in geographic region.

  Also, as far as a terminated employee goes, that employee is safest by not contacting clients that he or she gained while employed at your practice. If the employee has a contact list of clients from the your practice, the employee could become subject to liability by going through that list and contacting people, letting them know that he or she has left the company and is soliciting their business. The law draws a distinction between active solicitation and passive receipt of business, so while a former employee cannot actively solicit business, there's no restriction if a former client of his or hers calls from accepting that business.

  A client list is also a trade secret, and your business has the right to protect its trade secrets. Any business owner should include not only a non-solicitation provision, but also a provision that protects all your trade secrets, including your client lists. You will want to make sure all former employees return all company property, which includes client contact lists.

- **Can termination pay or severance contingent upon the employee signing a release be considered extortion?**
  It's not called extortion; however, you cannot withhold wages to which the employee is entitled in order to get the employee to sign a release. In that case, the release will be held void. For example, if the employee worked for two weeks and you say, "You can't have your paycheck unless you sign this release," that release is entirely void.

However, if you're talking about a severance, this is money that the employee is not otherwise entitled to, so you can hold that until you get a release or not give it at all if you choose.

DID YOU KNOW?

The Department of Labor estimates that over 70 percent of employers are noncompliant with the Fair Labor Standards Act. That means over 70 percent of employers in our country are walking cases for employment law liability. Additionally, over 30 percent of employers misclassify their employees as independent contractors.[4]

Chapter Four in Review

Hopefully, you learned to minimize liability in your tax practice by consulting with legal professionals and staying current with constantly evolving employment laws. This chapter discussed:

- **Properly classifying your employees.** There are three kinds of workers, including independent contractors, non-exempt employees, and exempt employees. Exempt employees could fall under the following categories:
  - Executive Exemption;
  - Administrative Exemption;
  - Learned Professional Exemption, which tax professionals are often considered to qualify for; and
  - Other less-used and specific exemptions.
- **Properly paying your employees.** Under federal law, overtime must be paid after 40 hours of work per week. States may require additional overtime under different circumstances.
- **Properly defining work weeks and work days.** Although an employer is able to set when a work week or day begins and ends, the following is concrete criteria:
  - A work week is seven consecutive days.
  - A work day is 24 consecutive hours.
  - Once a work week or day is set, it is very difficult to amend.
- **Avoiding disability and harassment claims.** What you don't know can't hurt you. Respect employee privacy, family matters, cultures, and differences.
- **Handling employee termination.** There are two kinds of employees you must consider before terminating: at-will employees and contract employees. At-will employees may be terminated at your discretion,

but you may be bound by rigid terms of employment for a contract employee. Consider severance packages for employees who may put you at-risk for liabilities.

- **Documenting the performance of all employees.** For-cause termination must be justified. Communicate conduct issues with your employees and document those conversations.

Familiarizing yourself with the employment laws of your state as well as federal laws will save you time, money and grief in the long run. Guarantee that you're doing everything in your practice to protect yourself, your employees, and your business from legal pursuit.

AFTERWORD

Whether you are looking to completely makeover your tax practice, improve its value for sale, or gain the freedom that owning a tax business is supposed to provide, I hope that you have found the answers to your staffing questions answered within these pages. Hiring, managing, and retaining employees can be challenging to say the least. Hopefully, you have acquired new tools through this book to successfully work with the current and prospective talent in your business.

There are so many new ideas and concepts I've presented that it may even seem overwhelming on how to start implementing innovative processes and improvements. Accordingly, in my closing thoughts, I would like to summarize a few of the key messages this book has presented.

Systematize Your Business!

To effectively run a successful tax practice, even in offices with no more than one employee, a systematic approach is crucial. Every function in a practice should be backed up by a concrete system. This is especially true if you are managing your practice to efficiently build your dream business.

Create and Use a TALENT Profile for Your Firm

Your business plan should present a clear idea of the direction of your business. Using this, you can begin to outline your needs for accomplishing your desired results. Hiring top talent for your tax business begins with a plan for hiring that corresponds to your desired results and goals. Using this TALENT profile enables you to evaluate potential candidates and even existing employees to ensure you are always working toward your desired outcome.

Always Scout

To convert your mentality in hiring from a reactive state of mind to a proactive one, never stop scouting for top talent for your tax business. Building a sufficient pool of candidates will allow you to hire for your needs ahead of time, not in reaction to an open position.

Make All Employment Decisions Based on Your TALENT Profile

Using your TALENT profile to make decisions in your tax practice applies for all decisions involving employment issues. When special requests are made by your current staff, consider how well they measure up to your TALENT profile when making your decisions. Your TALENT profile will act as a guide for your employment procedures to ensure that you stay true to the direction of your goals.

Properly Manage and Incentivize Your Team for Maximum Results

Managing staff to get the kind of results you really want in your business is going to help you get more done in less time with the kind of quality that you really want to deliver to your clients.

The Benefits of Systems in a Tax Practice

Implementing proper systems for all functions in your tax business will save you money, time, and headaches. The quality and accuracy of your office work will improve. You'll find increased communication and efficiency on all of your tax work, and the staff will be happier. This will improve office morale and as a result, your staff will perform better.

Incentivize, Measure and Hold Your Staff Accountable

There are six keys to a successful accountability system: provide your employees clear expectations, ensure your goals are primarily quantifiable, develop your accountability plan in advance, provide consequences and rewards, use signed performance contracts, and have regular, routine performance meetings. Clearly communicating expectations and holding your team accountable for its performance is half the battle in getting staff members to do what you want them to do. However, there is no point in accountability without measuring results.

Implement Performance Reviews

Self reviews, as well as supervisor assessments, are imperative for the performance review process. Using performance-based pay can be an excellent way to stretch your staffing budget and get better productivity from your talent.

Become Familiar with Labor Laws

Select a good employment attorney and develop a close relationship with someone who will keep you abreast of labor law changes affecting your business. Employment law is complicated and it is worth the expense and time to protect one of your biggest assets – your business.

Beware of Common Traps

Ignoring potential pitfalls you can encounter in the area of employment is similar to driving blind. Your ability to swerve and avoid colliding with objects on the road is only as good as your ability to see and anticipate a possible collision with that obstacle. Please pay close attention to the common traps I have outlined for you in each preceding chapter.

Additional Information

Following is an appendix with a listing of additional practice aids, templates, and tools available to members of Certified Tax Coach™. If you are interested in getting more information on how you can become a Certified Tax Coach™, please visit the AICTC™ website at www.CertifiedTaxCoach.org.

Contacting the Author

Dominique Molina is happy to receive any of your inquiries, questions, or feedback regarding this book and to discuss your tax business development needs. She frequently appears for speaking engagements, media interviews, and conferences. Her excellent media credentials, professionalism, and outgoing personality allow her to provide expert advice on tax issues to millions of taxpayers and tax business owners across the country. She can be reached at (877) 692-4282 or at admin@certifiedtaxcoach.com.

APPENDIX

Supplementary Materials for CTC™ Members

The following templates, samples, practice aids and tools are available to all Certified Tax Coach™ members to help give tax practices "Extreme Staff Makeovers." These materials, along with a special four-part video training on this topic can be found online in the CTC Toolbox™.

Practice Management Library

Attracting and Hiring Top Tax Talent

- Video of Workshop on Attracting and Hiring Top Tax Talent
- CTC™ Hiring System
- TALENT Profile Worksheet
- Sample TALENT Profile (completed)
- Sample Job Posting
- Sample of Response Cover Letter
- Sample Interview Agenda
- Sample Interview Questions
- Interview Rating System
- Sample Offer Letter
- Sample Rejection Letter

- Hiring Checklist
- Systems that Make Your Tax Business Soar!
- Video of Workshop on Systematizing Your Office
- Systems RoadMap
- 1040 Prep and Review Checklist
- 1065 and LLC Prep and Review Checklist
- 1120S Prep and Review Checklist
- 1120 Prep and Review Checklist
- Sample Tax Office Process – Docket

Accountability and Management

- Video of workshop on Managing Your Talent and Holding Them Accountable
- Employee Value Calculator
- Value of a Good Employee Sample
- Sample Performance Contract
- Self Review Questionnaire
- Sample Performance Review

Avoiding Employment Liability

- Video of Workshop on Employment Liability, featuring Guest Speaker, Bibianne Fell, Esq.
- Sample Warning Letter
- Sample Termination Letter

References

[1] http://www.hendersontraining.com/files/01Interview_Mistakes.pdf
[2] http://www.coffeeshopbusinessplanner.com/
[3] Carnegie Mellon Tepper School of Business
[4] Bibi Fell, Baker and McKenzie, LLP

ABOUT THE AUTHORS

Dominique Molina, CPA, CTC™

Dominique Molina is the co-founder and President of the American Institute of Certified Tax Coaches™. As the driving force and visionary behind the San Diego-based company, Ms. Molina set out to change the way tax professionals approach tax planning. In 2009, Ms. Molina began to create an elite network of tax professionals including CPAs, EAs, attorneys, and financial service providers who are trained to help their clients proactively plan and implement tax strategies that can rescue thousands of dollars in wasted tax. Her more than 12 years of hands-on experience in the accounting and business fields provide her with ample skills to accomplish this mission. Ms. Molina has successfully licensed tax professionals as Certified Tax Coaches across the country, creating a national network of highly qualified professionals who provide proactive service for their clients. This premier group of professionals features less than 200 specialists in 40 states who have achieved this very specialized designation.

Prior to founding Certified Tax Coach™, Ms. Molina successfully managed her own practice, AccountOnIt, a San Diego-based, full-service tax, accounting, and business consulting firm, serving hundreds of business owners and investors across the country for seven years. Preceding this, Ms. Molina assisted a variety of clients for the largest independently-owned CPA firm in San Diego.

Ms. Molina received her bachelor's degree in Accounting from San Diego State University. Upon graduation, she began her accounting work as a staff accountant, controller, and office manager at several closely-held asset management and investment companies, including Segue Capital, Inc., and RMC Capital Management, Inc.

Ms. Molina frequently appears as a tax expert and TV guest in regional television markets, including San Diego and Los Angeles. Her excellent media credentials, professionalism, and outgoing personality allow her to provide expert advice on tax issues for thousands of Southern Californians. Ms. Molina is also a published author of two books on taxation, and has written a foreword for one of our country's preeminent tax books. Her latest co-authored book, Breaking the Tax Code, is set for release in January 2011. A frequent lecturer and speaker, Ms. Molina often teaches at Professional Association of Small Business Accountants conferences, and instructs continuing professional education for CPE Link. Her website also receives thousands of visitors per month who follow her financial video blogs.

When not solving the challenges of America's taxpayers, Ms. Molina loves being a wife and a mother. She spends her free time with her family, enjoying San Diego, surfing, tennis, reading, traveling and running. Ms. Molina is also a classical pianist.

Bibianne U. Fell, Esq.

Bibianne Fell is an adjunct professor and regular guest lecturer at the University of San Diego, School of Law and serves on the faculty of the National Institute of Trial Advocacy. Ms. Fell is also a graduate of the American Board of Trial Advocates Trial College and was selected by the San Diego Daily Transcript as a Top Young Attorney.

Ms. Fell handles a wide range of employment matters including sexual harassment, discrimination, and wage and hour class action cases before federal and state courts and administrative agencies including the Equal Employment Opportunity Commission, Department of Fair Employment and Housing, and the Employment Development Department. Several of Ms. Fell's cases have been reported as precedential opinions. Ms. Fell also conducts employment compliance audits for companies of all sizes, advises employers and human resource professionals on employment law issues, and is a regular guest speaker at employment law seminars.

After working at Baker & McKenzie for several years, handling both general civil and employment law matters, she and George Fleming left to form Fleming PC. Fleming PC is a litigation and employment law boutique which offers its clients big firm quality, with small firm flexibility. Fleming PC has been selected by U.S. News and World Reports as a First Tier Law Firm in San Diego.

Ms. Fell graduated magna cum laude from the University of San Diego, School of Law, where she was a member of the Law Review and was elected to the Order of the Coif. During law school, Ms. Fell received the 2004 CALI Award for Excellence in Advanced Trial Advocacy and the Outstanding Oral Advocate Award. Ms. Fell graduated cum laude from the University of California, San Diego with a degree in Political Science.

Made in the USA
Lexington, KY
31 May 2011